Srimad Bhagavatam

The Wisdom of God

TRANSLATED BY
SWĀMI PRABHAVĀNANDA

SRI RAMAKRISHNA MATH
MYLAPORE, MADRAS

Published by
Adhyaksha
Sri Ramakrishna Math
#31, Ramakrishna Mutt Road,
Mylapore, Chennai–600004

Originally published by
The Vedanta Society of Southern California,
Hollywood, USA

Ninth edition, First print, January 2023
2000 copies

ISBN: 978-81-7823-315-4

For distribution in India only

Printed in India at
Sri Ramakrishna Math Printing Press
Mylapore, Chennai-4

PREFACE

AFTER the Upanishads and the Bhagavadgīta, the Śrīmad Bhāgavatam is the most authoritative of the Indian Scriptures. By means of stories from the lives of Avatāras, sages, devotees, and kings, it popularizes the truths contained in the Vedas. At this moment more than two hundred million Hindus find in it their most cherished expressions of religious faith and their dearest exemplars. To study it is the best of all ways to become acquainted with the living religion of India.

Its peculiar excellence is that it reconciles the heart with the head, devotion with learning. " It is fried in the butter of Knowledge," says Śrī Rāmakriṣṇa, latest of Indiain prophets, " and steeped in the honey of Love."

Only the more generally interesting portions of the work—amounting to somewhat less than half of the whole—are included in the present version. Of this version, again, about half is summary and paraphrase rather than translation ; the remainder, however, consisting of the teachings of Śrī Kriṣṇa to his disciple Uddhava (Book XI), has been rendered without omission and with approximate literalness. Everywhere the primary object has been to interpret in English the inner spirit of the Sanskrit text.

In no form hitherto, so far as I am aware, has the Bhāgavatam been readily available to the English-speaking public.

In revising my translation for the press, I am happy to acknowledge, I have had the assistance of my friends Jane Manchester and Frederick Manchester.

PRABHAVANANDA

CONTENTS

BOOK FIRST

THE ARGUMENT

A COMPANY of sages ask a well-known Sūta,[1] to teach them spiritual truths and to tell them of the divine incarnation of Śrī Krișṇa. After speaking for a time from his own wisdom, Sūta tells of the *Bhāgavatam*—of how Vyāsa came to compose this holy book, of how he taught it to his son Śuka, and of how Śuka in turn, when King Parīkṣit was about to die, related it to the saintly monarch. The Sūta was present when Śuka appeared before King Parīkṣit, and so is able to narrate all that happened on that blessed occasion. This he here begins to do, describing the reverence with which Śuka was received and the request which the king made of him.

CHAPTER I

SŪTA COMES TO THE FOREST OF NAIMIṢA

IN very ancient times there lived in the forest of Naimiṣa several great sages. One day

[1] Sūta : one of a class of saintly minstrels who recited and explained Purānic texts. The Sūta in question is Ugraśravas the son of Romaharṣaṇa.

while they were sitting together, after their morning ablutions, prayers and meditations, there came to them a well-known Sūta, Ugraśravas by name. The sages were very much pleased to see him. They welcomed him with due respect and reverently addressed him thus :

" O sinless one, thou art indeed a free soul. Through the Grace of thy Guru, the spirit of all the Scriptures is known to thee ; therefore may it please thee to reveal unto us the teachings that would be of benefit to all mankind. Tell us also, we pray thee, what thou knowest of the sacred life of the divine incarnation of Śrī Krișņa. We know that the Lord of the universe, for his pleasure and play, and for the salvation of mankind, assumes different forms in different ages. Men become holy by singing the praises of the Lord and by telling of his divine deeds and pastimes.

" Even by uttering his sacred name, one gains freedom from the deep mire of ignorance, and becomes fearless. Such a one Fear dares not approach.

" By surrendering themselves to the Feet of the Lord, the self-controlled Munis become so perfect that even those who merely associate with them grow pure and holy.

" The sacred river Ganges sanctifies everyone, because she springs from the Feet of the Lord.

" Indeed, simply to listen to accounts of his divine work and play is purifying. All this we know : but we would fain hear more."

Assenting to their request, the great, saintly Sūta thus replied :

" O revered sages, there is nothing greater or more purifying than to converse about God and his divine play. The highest religion of man is unselfish love of God. If one has this love, one attains to truly divine wisdom. Fruitless is that knowledge which is not love. Fruitless is religion itself, if it have not love. Vain indeed is all struggle for spiritual life if in one's heart there be not love.

" Religion is not for the purpose of securing a place in heaven. It is an inquiry into Truth, and its ideal is the knowledge and the realization of Truth.

" The knowers of Truth call Truth the infinite, eternal knowledge. The followers of the Vedas call it Brahman, the worshippers of Hiranyagarbha call it the Universal Spirit, and devotees call it God.

" The self-controlled Munis, with faith and reverence in their hearts, having realized true love, find that universal Self within themselves. And it is found, O great sages, whatever the religion or the path that is followed, he alone is blessed who pleases the Lord within, and who has love for him.

"God is the refuge and strength of all. One ought, therefore, to hear about Him, sing His praises, worship Him, and meditate upon Him. To the wise, meditation is like a sword to sever the knots of all evil Karma.

"A man of good deeds, living in association with holy men gradually acquires faith in religion.

"When faith comes, there arises the desire to hear the Word of God. When the desire to hear the Word of God arises, one finds pleasure in his Word. When one finds pleasure in his Word, all evils vanish. For then the Lord, the friend of the godly, reveals Himself and wipes away all evils and impurities.

"When all impurities are washed away, then comes true, unswerving love of God. In minds so purified there cannot arise any thought of lust or greed ; and their joy is full.

"When the joy of devotion to the Lord takes hold of the mind, man frees himself from the bondage of the world. He realizes the Truth and knows the Self. His ego is dissolved. His doubts vanish. For such a man bondage to Karma ceases.

"Hence the wise should always love the Lord and find joy in Him.

"The ideal to which all the Vedas point, the goal of all sacrifices and Yogas, of all work, knowledge, and austerities, the very truth of all religions, is the Lord of Love. There is no other goal but He.

"The Lord, though without form and attributes, and beyond all Guṇas, projected this universe out of his divine Māyā. Having brought forth this universe, He dwells within all beings and within all things. Yet He remains unaffected, for He is pure consciousness.

"As water, though one and formless when poured into different vessels assumes many shapes according to the shapes of the vessels, so the Lord, the soul of the universe, takes on the appearance of various objects. The Lord of Love, for his pleasure and play, has assumed the myriad forms of gods, men, animals, birds, and of all other things animate and inanimate. Infinite is the Lord and infinite are His expressions.

"But Śrī Kriṣṇa, the embodiment of love and divinity, is His special manifestation.

"Whenever the Truth is forgotten in the world, and wickedness prevails, the Lord becomes flesh to show the way, the Truth, and the life to humanity. Such an incarnation is an Avatāra, an embodiment of God on earth.

"Man is divine. He is, in reality, the impersonal Truth. His essential nature is pure consciousness. Bound by Māyā, he ignorantly thinks of himself as the gross human form.

"Just as clouds, hanging in the air, are by the ignorant attributed to the sky ; just as the dust of the earth, when raised by the wind, is by the ignorant attributed to the ether ; so are body and mind attributed by the ignorant to the impersonal Self.

"There is the gross physical body. There is also the subtle body, consisting of mind, intellect, and ego. These bodies together are called the adjuncts of the spirit, of the impersonal Self. When, through ignorance, man thinks the spirit to be identical with these adjuncts, he is bound by his deeds, good and bad.

"When he acquires knowledge and perceives these gross and subtle bodies to be adjuncts, separate from the real Self, he realizes Brahman and is free. He becomes Brahman and shines blissfully in his own glory.

" The omniscient Lord, though beyond birth and the bondage of Karma, assumes human birth from choice, and is manifested as Krișṇa or Rāma. There is a great difference between such a divine incarnation and an ordinary man. For the former, though born as man, is born free and with knowledge. Though apparently limited by personality, He knows Himself to be impersonal and indwelling spirit in all beings. Like an actor on the stage, He remains unaffected by the role He plays.

" Difficult indeed is it for the ignorant to understand His glory and power. Only those who with love and devotion worship and meditate at the blessed Feet of a divine incarnation can realize the Truth.

" O ye sages, blessed indeed are ye, for ye love the Lord. Who so loves him is free indeed.

" O revered sages, I will now tell you of the *Bhāgavatam* as I have heard it. It was compiled by the great sage Vyāsa, and gives in brief form the teachings of all the Scriptures. Vyāsa taught the *Bhāgavatam* to Śuka, his son, a young man of wisdom and great fame, who in turn taught it to King Parīkṣit. The royal sage, surrounded by many learned Brahmins, sat in meditation, with the object of yielding up his body, and listened devoutly to the holy Word."

Śaunaka, the eldest of the sages, at the mention of Śuka's name could no longer remain silent.

"Revered master," he said, "pray tell us of that book of God which Śuka taught. When and how did Vyāsa compile it? It is interesting to know that Śuka was the first to give out its teachings. Śuka, the son of Vyāsa, was indeed a great Yogi, a knower of Brahman, who realized unity in the midst of diversity. His mind and consciousness were always united with God. We have heard about him, and how, after beginning the life of renunciation, having no consciousness of his body, he would walk about naked. One day, while thus walking in the wood, he passed by a lake in which some nymphs were bathing. They watched him pass, feeling no shyness in his presence; but as Vyāsa, who was following his son, approached, they hastily got out of the water and clothed themselves. This surprised the great sage, and he asked the nymphs, 'Why do you act so strangely, my children? You did not shrink from the young Śuka, who was naked, yet you feel shy before me, an old man, fully clothed.' To this the nymphs replied: 'Revered sir, in you there lingers a trace of the consciousness of sex, but in your son Śuka there is none'."

Thus again importuned, the Sūta willingly consented to the desire of the sages, and beginning his long story told first, in loving detail, of how Vyāsa resolved to write the *Bhāgavatam* and of how he taught it to his son, the holy Śuka.

CHAPTER II

VYĀSA AND NĀRADA

THE great sage Vyāsa, while sitting in meditation at the Badarika Āśrama in the Himalayas, saw in spiritual vision that a great change was approaching, an epochal change, and that with this change people were likely to become more worldly and to forget all spiritual truths. He pondered deeply upon this, and speculated as to what could be done to help humanity. At last, after much thought and meditation, he decided to bring together the Vedas. As a first step he made of them four groups, and so taught them to his disciples. Then, to adapt the teachings of the Vedas to the understanding of all, he wrote the great epic, the Mahābhārata.

All this he did for the good of humanity, but even then his heart was not satisfied. He felt that his mission was incomplete and that the world was in need of something more. One day, while he was still pondering what further he could do to serve humanity, the great sage Nārada appeared before him. Vyāsa, reflecting that he might receive comfort from the sage, thus began :

O most honoured sage, though I have attained to the highest Truth, and the fullness of life, my heart is sad for humanity. You, who are a sage of great wisdom, know the thoughts of all. Please tell me how I can bring Truth to mankind.

Nārada :

Vyāsa, you are the wisest man of the age. The world is in need of another great book of wisdom from you. Write it so that every verse will sing the glory of the Lord and instill a great love for Him into the hearts of men. For your subject take the great truth—there is none greater—that in the liberated soul love and knowledge are at last reconciled, and for the perfect illustration of this truth tell again the story of the divine life of Śrī Krișṇa, the God of Love. Divine love, which delivers us from all evils and from all impurities, is supreme. Supreme love and supreme wisdom are one. Sing, then, the glories of the Lord, sing His praises, that the Lord at once of wisdom and of love may abide in the hearts of all who read or hear your words and may bestow upon them His everlasting peace.

Let me now tell of my past incarnation, and of how I came to find this divine freedom and peace which I have. My mother was a servant in a retreat where great sages lived. I was reared in close association with them, and I too served them. While I was thus living in the society of these holy men, my heart was purified. These sages were always singing the glory and praise of the Lord ; I used to hear them, and thus in my heart grew great love for the Lord, and I became devoted to Him. One day the sages, because of their love for me, initiated me into the sacred mysteries of wisdom. The veil of ignorance was removed from me, and I knew my real Self as divine.

Then I learned this lesson, that the greatest remedy for all the ills of life, physical or mental, is to surrender the fruits of all our Karmas to the Lord. Karma places us in bondage, but by resigning our Karma to the Lord we are freed. Work which we perform as service to the Lord creates love and devotion in us. This love and devotion, in turn, bring wisdom, and at last guided by this wisdom, we surrender ourselves to the Lord of Love and meditate upon Him. Thus it was that I attained to wisdom and love ; and now I desire that you should sing the glory and praise of God, that all who hear may find, as I have found, eternal happiness and freedom.

Vyāsa :

Continue, O Nārada, I pray you, the story of your life.

Nārada :

I lived with the sages until my mother died, when I left the retreat and wandered about, visiting various countries, towns, and cities. At last I went into a deep forest in search of solitude. Seated under a tree, in a quiet, lonely place, I remembered what the sages had taught me, that God dwells within the heart. So there, forgetting the world in the love of the Lord, I meditated upon Him. Gradually, as my inner vision became clear, I saw the benign Lord of Love seated in the sanctuary of my heart. I was overwhelmed with joy inexpressible, for I could no longer think of myself as separate from God—I had discovered my identity with Him. But not for long was I to remain in that state. Again I found myself in the world of the senses ; and now, alas, when with all eagerness I sought to reach once more that state of blessedness, it seemed impossible for me to do so. Then I heard a voice from the void. The Lord was speaking as if to console me : " My child, you will not see Me again in this life. Those who have not their desires quenched cannot see Me ; but because of your devotion to Me, I vouchsafed that experience to you once. Saints devoted to Me gradually give up all desires. Live in the company of the holy, attend upon them, and fix your mind firmly on Me. Thus you will ultimately realize your unity with Me. Then will there be no more separation for you, nor will there be for you any more death or destruction."

I bowed down in reverence and gratitude. After that, I wandered about in many countries, chanting His name, meditating on Him, and singing His glory and praise.

In due time I gave up the body and became united with the Lord. I lived in that blessedness of union for a whole cycle.[1] In the beginning of the next cycle I was sent forth into this world, where, now living a life of purity

[1] The visible universe, according to the Hindu conception, comes into being, endures for a time, and finally dissolves—only again, after an interval, to repeat the same process. When the universe starts to evolve, a cycle begins ; when it dissolves, the cycle ends.

and continence, I can wander about everywhere, in every Loka, through the grace of the Lord. Wherever I go, I play on my Vīṇā and sing the praises of the Lord, and the Lord of Love is always manifest in my heart. Those who hear my songs in praise of the Lord find peace and freedom.

Nārada, having ended the story of his life, took leave of Vyāsa and went away.

After Nārada had departed, the great sage Vyāsa went to Śamyāprāsa, the holy retreat on the bank of the Saraswatī. There, as he sat for meditation, his mind became deeply concentrated through love for the Lord, and he beheld the Father-Mother God Omnipotent. He realized how man, though divine and free, through ignorance believes himself bound, but also how through devotion to Śrī Krisṇa the Lord of Love, this ignorance can be dispelled. With this truth in his heart he wrote the Sacred Book, the *Bhāgavatam*, for the good of mankind. He then taught this wisdom to his son Śuka, who was born pure, and free from all attachment.

I must now tell you something about King Parīkṣit, the grandson of Arjuna, and about the circumstances under which Śuka met the King and taught him the *Bhāgavatam*.

CHAPTER III

KING PARĪKSIT MEETS KALI

ONE day King Parīkṣit, ruler of all India, while standing on the bank of the river Sarasvatī, saw a man tormenting and ill-treating a bull and a cow. Such cruelty angered the king. He asked the man to explain his cowardly behaviour, telling him at the same time that it was within his royal power to punish him for such conduct by death. Then, not waiting for a reply, the king turned his attention to the animals, which were still shivering with fear, and spoke to them with such kindness that he soon inspired them with confidence and trust.

While the king was pondering the plight of the bull, wondering who could have cut off his legs, the bull, who was the personification of virtue, spoke as follows :

" Your Majesty, we thank you for your kind protection. You are curious to know the cause of my suffering, but what it is I do not know. There are many different opinions about the true cause of pain and suffering in this world. Some say we ourselves cause our own happiness and suffering ; others say the stars or planetary conditions are the causes — or, peradventure, fate ; again others say Karma is the only cause. Still others think that God sends us either happiness or misery. I am at a loss to know which of these views is correct."

Hearing a bull speak, the king was amazed. Then, as he pondered deeply on the words uttered, a veil seemed to be removed from his sight, and he recognized the bull as the personification of virtue, the cow as the personification of mother earth, and the man who was tormenting them as Kali, the personification of the iron age, or vice.

Then he addressed the bull, saying :

" You are indeed the personification of virtue. You have assumed the form of a bull. Your four feet are austerity, purity, charity, and truthfulness ; but when doubt, attachment and pride entered into the world, you lost three feet. Now you are standing on one foot, which is truthfulness, and this man, Kali, the personification of the iron age, was about to crush this foot also."

So saying, he turned to Kali with drawn sword, ready to kill him ; but Kali fell at his feet asking for pardon and safety, knowing that a king cannot kill any creature that sues for his protection. The king stayed his hand, but commanded Kali to leave his kingdom. Kali then asked the king to give over to him all the parts of his realm where flourished the four vices of gambling, drinking, inhuman treatment of women and cruelty to animals. This request the king granted. Then Kali, wishing to extend his realm, asked for still more territory, whereupon the king offered him in addition the domains of falsehood, pride, lust, jealousy, and enmity.

Hence, if a man would not be overpowered by Kali, he must shun these evils.

The king then restored the legs of the bull, leaving him steadfast in the virtues of austerity, purity, charity and truthfulness.

CHAPTER IV

KING PARĪKṢIT IS CURSED

ONE day while King Parīkṣit was hunting in a deep forest he became very thirsty, and as he wandered about in search of water he discovered the retreat of the well-known saint Śamīka. The saint was sitting quietly, with eyes closed, in deep meditation, his senses, mind, and intellect under perfect control. He was neither awake, nor dreaming, nor asleep. He was in Samādhi, that state of consciousness wherein one realizes one's unity with Brahman.

There was no movement in his limbs. His body was perfectly still.

The king saw the saint thus, but did not recognize his condition, and being very thirsty he asked for a drink of water. The saint Śamīka neither saw him nor heard his request. Thereupon the king, thinking that the saint was deliberately ignoring him, became very angry. After waiting impatiently for some response, he suddenly picked up a dead snake which was lying near by and angrily threw it onto the neck of the saint, who was still in deep Samādhi. He then walked rapidly away.

Now this saint had a son named Śringī, who was born endowed with great power. When he learned of the indignity which the king had inflicted upon his father and saw the snake still hanging on his neck, he became enraged, and bursting into tears cursed the king saying: "The king must pay heavily for this insult to my father. Seven days hence he shall die of the bite of a snake."

When the saint awoke from his meditation he saw his son weeping. He said gently, "Why do you cry, my son; has anyone harmed you?"

The boy then related the whole incident to his father. When the saint learned of the curse, he was very sorrowful, and said, "My son, one wrong is not corrected by another. And now, alas, the curse cannot be revoked; a Brahmin's word once given cannot be recalled. Let the Lord play as he will. Everything is in his hands."

CHAPTER V

KING PARĪKṢIT MEETS ŚUKA

WHEN King Parīkṣit returned home, he was filled with remorse because of his mistreatment of the saint. He soon learned of the fatal curse which Śringī had called down upon him, and it gladdened his heart, for it seemed to him a blessing in disguise. "I shall be free from my misdeeds," he said to himself. "Furthermore, the thought of death will cure me of my great attachment to temporal pleasures and powers. I have become more and more devoted to the world, and now I shall fill the remainder of my days with the thought of the Lord."

Then the king bestowed his kingdom and all his possessions upon his son Janamejaya, and went to live on the bank of the sacred river Ganges for the purpose of meeting his end peacefully, with his mind absorbed in the thought of Śrī Krisṇa, the God of Love. Many holy men came to him, and he asked for their blessings. " I bow down at the feet of all holy Brahmins," he said. " Bless me that I may have more and more love for the infinite Lord. Whatever different birth I may undergo hereafter, may I associate always with holy men and true lovers of God. This is my only prayer."

As his mind became free from all worldly attachment, and his heart purified by desire for the love of God, he felt peaceful and calm. While he was surrounded by holy men, and conversing on God, Śuka, the son of Vyāsa, came into that assembly. Śuka, though only sixteen years of age, was old in knowledge and wisdom. His form was of an ineffable grace and beauty. His face glowed, and his eyes shone as if from gazing into the infinite. He had no caste mark on him, nor any clothing. Indeed, he could roam about free as the birds of the air, for he was truly a knower of Brahman.

As he approached the assembly, all stood up in reverence. King Parīkṣit, after prostrating himself at the feet of Śuka, with folded hands said, " O great master, as you have blessed me with your holy presence, pray teach me the duties of a man desiring freedom. Teach me how to find God."

Thus requested, Śuka, who knew all religions and all truths, began to teach him.

BOOK SECOND

THE ARGUMENT

THE Sūta, continuing his narrative, reports the words of Śuka as, from his own wisdom, he taught King Parīkṣit.

CHAPTER I

WORSHIP AND MEDITATION

O KING, blessed indeed are you to have developed this desire for Truth and freedom. Very few there are who even inquire concerning these things. Most people are busily engaged in obtaining creature comforts only, and spend their energy chiefly in providing for themselves and their families. Even though it is the universal experience that everything in this world vanishes away, yet do they remain attached to the dream of earthly life, forgetting that the Lord alone abideth for ever.

It is the great use and glory of human birth that to man the power is given to discriminate between the Self and the non-Self, and to practise the Ashṭāngayoga ; and it is the highest goal of human life to be united in consciousness with the God of Love.

Blessed indeed are those moments of our lives when we think of God and worship him ; all other time is idly spent. Vain are all things and of no account, except to love God.

Shun all fear of death. Cut the ties of the world with the sharp sword of renunciation.

Seated in a secluded place, free from all disturbing thoughts of the world, one must first repeat in one's mind the sacred word OM, with understanding of its meaning. The word OM is one with God, and indeed is God. By this practice alone one gains control of Prāṇa and of the mind. With the discriminative faculty as guide, one should, with the help of the mind, draw the senses and the sense-organs completely away from the objects of the world. Let the devotee now meditate upon the Lord. Let him be absorbed in him. When absorption comes, there arises a great calmness, a transcendental bliss. That is the Supreme goal, the abode of Viṣṇu, the kingdom of heaven.

If for any reason the mind becomes restless again, being overpowered by Rajas or deluded by Tamas, let it be brought again under control by the practice of concentration. This practice alone washes away all the impurities arising from Rajas or Tamas. The seers, the Yogis, perfected in the art of concentration, find great joy in spiritual life, and ultimately become one with universal love.

A wise man, though living in the world, is never attached to it. Neither does he seek to gratify his senses, for he knows that in the pleasures of senses there is no true happiness. Nor does he spend his energy in seeking bodily comforts. He sleeps on the lap of the earth, mother of all ; the sky is his roof, the grass his bed. Nature supplies him with food ; rivers provide his drink. He worships not the riches of the earth, nor yet the rich, intoxicated as they are by the power of wealth.

The God of Love exists in the heart of all. He is our very Self, and therefore very dear to us. He is Truth. He is infinity. He is the omnipotent Lord. Hence should a man, freed from all selfish desires, his mind fixed on God, worship him alone.

Do thou, O king, meditate on him within the shrine of thine own heart, and lose thyself in the consciousness of the Divine Being.

CHAPTER II

THE ATTAINMENT OF FREEDOM

A TRUE Yogi realizing the approach of death sits calmly in Yoga posture, and, with his heart purified and mind under perfect control, becomes absorbed in the consciousness of Brahman. Thus he lives in a state of perfect tranquility.

Time, the great destroyer, which lords it over everything in the universe, is annihilated. The universe itself melts into nothingness. The Yogi is no longer aware of his physical self. The worshipful Lord Viṣṇu alone is in his heart. All to him is God. Such is his blissful state.

Desiring to give up the body, he allows the vital energy to pass through the different centres of consciousness. First, the energy is concentrated in the solar plexus, called the Maṇipūra. From there the energy rises to Anāhata, the heart. It then passes to the centre near the throat, called the Viśuddha. From there it ascends to Ājnā, the centre between the eyebrows.

At this point one of two things may come to pass. If the Yogi has reached the state of desirelessness, he realizes the absolute

Brahman, and the vital energy ascends to the Sahasrāra the thousand-petalled lotus-centre in the brain, called the doorway to Brahman. Then the Yogi, realizing his unity with Brahman, completes the separation of himself from the senses, the sense-organs, the mind, and the body and passes away. He attains to what is known as absolute freedom. This is called immediate liberation.

If, having raised his vital energy to the centre between the eyebrows, the Yogi, on the other hand, still has some desires left in him, he does not realize the absolute unity, but passes away still associating himself with the mind and the senses. He then ascends to higher and higher Lokas, and ultimately reaches the Brahma-Loka. There he becomes freed from all desires and realizes his unity with Brahman; and thus, having attained absolute freedom, there is for him no more return. This is called the gradual liberation.

Be ye therefore, O King, a Yogi, for by worshipping the Lord of Love one has all desires fulfilled and in the end attains freedom. Even hearing of God stimulates the higher consciousness and brings about detachment from the fleeting world. So should a man follow the path of freedom, the path of love. Blessed indeed is his life on earth who devotes himself to the worship of the Lord.

CHAPTER III

ŚUKA'S PRAYER TO THE LORD

O THOU Lord supreme, I bow down to thee !
For thy sole pleasure and play didst thou bring forth this Universe.
Thou art the highest in the highest ! Who can sing thine infinite glory ?
Thou art the innermost ruler of every heart ;
Thy paths are mysterious ;
Thy ways are blessed.
Thou dost wipe away all the tears of thy devotees ;
Thou dost destroy the wickedness of the wicked.
Thy form is purity itself, and thou dost give purity and Self-knowledge to those who seek thee.
Salutations to thee again and again, O Lord of hosts !

I praise thee, O Lord !
Thou art the strength and support of all thy worshippers ;

Thou art manifest in the hearts of all true
Yogis ;
The evildoer findeth thee not.
Thou art One without a second.
Thou dost shine in thine own glory, in thy
resplendent, blissful Self.
What sweetness is in thy name.
What joy is in thy remembrance !
Those who chant thy holy name, and meditate
on thee, become for ever free from all evils ;
The wise, worshipping thy Feet, conquer all
fear of life and death :
Thus do they realize thee, thou supreme goal
of all true seekers.
Before thee there is no barrier of caste, or
race, or creed ;
All thy children attain purity through thy
holy name.
Calm souls worship thee, knowing that they
are one with thee.
Thou art the Lord supreme,
Thou art indeed the Vedas,
Thou art the Truth,
Thou art the goal of all discipline ;
Thy lovers meditate on thy blissful form, and
become lost in the joy thereof.
Shower thy grace upon me, O Lord, and in
thy mercy look upon me !

Thou art the Lord of wealth.
Thou art the Lord of all creation.
The Lord of all thy lovers and devotees.
Look upon all beings with thy mercy!
Blessed are they that meditate on thy Lotus Feet,
For they shall be purified:
Blessed are they that are purified,
For they shall attain Self-knowledge.
The wise call thee the impersonal, without attributes;
They also call thee personal God with divine attributes:
Thou art both, and thou dost manifest thyself as the one or the other,
According to our understanding.
O Lord, forever look in mercy upon me!

Yes, continued Śuka, addressing King Parīkṣit, the Lord is the embodiment of Tapas, and only by practising Tapas may be realized. It is said that when Brahmā was desirous of creating, he sought anxiously to learn through what knowledge he could acquire the necessary power. While he was thus engaged, he heard a voice from the void saying: 'Tapa.' He started at the sound and looked around for the speaker, but seeing no one he understood it to be the voice of God.

So in accordance with the command of the Lord he began to practise Tapas by controlling the breath, the organs of sense, and the mind. This he did for many, many years.

At last God, pleased with Brahmā's faithful and unswerving devotion to Tapas, revealed unto him the Vaikuṇtha, the heavenly abode, where there is no sorrow, neither any fear. Brahmā then saw God in his true nature, whereupon the Lord of Love addressed him thus :

" O thou First-Created, I am indeed well pleased with thee. The highest good, the supreme goal, is to know me as I am. Through my grace hast thou known me, and known my highest abode.

" O thou sinless one, when thou didst hear the voice saying unto thee 'Tapa,' it was I who spoke. Tapas is my heart ; yea, even my very soul. By the power of Tapas alone do I create, preserve, and destroy this universe. Tapas is my strength. Before this universe came to be, I was. When the universe shall have passed away, I shall be. At the heart of the universe, throughout the cycle of its existence, I am. I am all this. Eternal—without beginning, without end—I am."

Therefore, O king, one must practise Tapas, if one would know the Truth.

BOOK THIRD

THE ARGUMENT

SUTA, continuing his narrative, tells how Śuka began to teach to King Parīkṣit the holy *Bhāgavatam*, and repeats after him its opening chapters. In these chapters Maitreya relates to Vidura the story of creation and the lives of Manu, Śatarūpā, and Kapila—the first of mankind.

CHAPTER I

VIDURA AND MAITREYA

Now, continued Śuka, I will begin the teachings of the most sacred *Bhāgavatam* by relating the conversation between Vidura and Maitreya.

Vidura and Maitreya, sages of great fame, were disciples of Śrī Kriṣṇa. Vidura renounced the world in his early youth and wandered about to many places of pilgrimage. His mind was always steadfast in the thought of the Lord of Love. He was a free soul, perfected in the love of God. Maitreya was also a free soul, learned in divine wisdom.

Once during his wanderings Vidura visited Maitreya, who was then living at Hardwar. As soon as they met, their hearts melted in divine love for each other. They spent many happy days together, conversing on God.

One day Vidura, musing, said:

O great sage, although men are always running about in search of happiness, suffering is their unhappy lot. Can anything be done to remedy this? Pray tell me, what would bring the greatest good to humanity.

There are people who, because of their bad Karmas from the past, engage in evil pursuits and devote no time to the thought or worship of God. For this reason they suffer. But saints such as you, O Maitreya, devoted to the love of God alone, live in this world solely for the good of humanity. Pray teach me that eternal knowledge whereby God and his love may be revealed in the hearts of all, that they may find eternal happiness.

Tell me also about the creation of this universe. It is interesting to learn how God—the one absolute existence—became manifold.

As a bee gathers honey from many different flowers, so have you gathered the essence of all Scriptures, and you should reveal it for the benefit of mankind.

Maitreya :

O blessed Vidura, I thank you for this inquiry, and for the tribute you pay me.

The creation, preservation, and dissolution of the universe are all divine play. In the universe, the Self, who is the Self of all beings, appears as many. Before creation, and in dissolution, the world exists as one absolute existence, which is God. Then there is neither the seer nor the seen, neither subject nor object. There exists only consciousness itself. In that consciousness, which is the absolute God, is the power which divides itself into the seer and the seen, the cause and the effect. This power is called Māyā.

God created this universe out of his Māyā, the divine power, which consists of the three Guṇas, namely, Sattva, Rajas, and Tamas. This Māyā, consisting of the Guṇas, is also called Avyakta—which is to say " nature not yet manifested." Mind, intelligence, ego senses, sense organs, subtle elements, and gross elements—in short, the whole universe—are an emanation from the divine Māyā.

Vidura :

Revered master, if that is so, how can God, who is consciousness itself, and unchangeable, be called the Creator? And why should he create? If we say that for his pleasure and play he created this universe, we give him feelings like our own. When children engage in play, they are prompted by desire; but how can God, who is perfect, have any desire?

If, as you say, the absolute impersonal God is not really the Creator, but it is his power, Māyā, which creates, preserves, and dissolves, how can this Māyā be associated with God? Furthermore, man, or the individual spirit, is in reality God, or part of God. How does he then become associated with and bound by this Māyā? Man is truly divine. How then is he ever deluded, and why does he grovel in misery?

Maitreya:

Man, the ever-free Lord, is never bound; but man's belief that he is bound is Māyā, and, because of this Māyā, the unreal appears to be real. When the moon is reflected on the ocean, the waves of the ocean make it appear restless, but in reality the moon is steady and calm. It is the water that is restless. Similarly, the attributes of the non-Self are superimposed upon the Self, and it is the ignorant man who, through Māyā, identifies the attributes of finitude and bondage with himself. But this bondage is never in the true Self.

When by following the path of renunciation one becomes pure, the grace of the divine Self, and devotion to the Lord, and love for him, arise within one's heart. Then does one know himself to be ever free. In short, when a man loves God, he frees himself from all ignorance and from all misery.

Vidura:

I thank you, O Maitreya. The true nature of God, as well as of man, is consciousness itself. I was puzzled as to why God remains forever free and is the ruler of the universe, whereas man finds himself bound. But now I understand that Māyā is the servant of God, whereas it is the master of man. Herein lies the explanation of man's bondage. I also understand how ignorance, which is the cause of all this apparent universe, itself is Māyā.

Indeed, here as elsewhere, extremes resemble each other. The most ignorant man is happy, and likewise the most enlightened man—each in his own fashion. But those who are midway, being neither completely ignorant nor completely enlightened, are wretched. They have realized the ephemeral nature of the world and are dissatisfied with its pleasures, yet they do not know of the bliss of God.

It is only by associating with holy men such as you, O Maitreya, and by rendering service to them, that men can develop love for the Lord and in the end find in him both joy and peace.

O most honoured sage, I understand that the universe is a work of the Divine Power. Pray relate the story of Creation, and of how beings and things came into existence.

CHAPTER II

THE STORY OF CREATION

Maitreya :

CREATION, O Vidura, has no absolute beginning. The present universe is but one of a series of worlds that are past and of worlds that are to be. The cosmic energy alternates between periods of potentiality and of expression. The phase of potentiality is known as dissolution ; the phase of expression is known as creation.

Created things are of different kinds. The Avyakta, or cosmic energy, consists of three Guṇas. When the equilibrium of the Guṇas is disturbed, there are manifested universal intelligence, universal ego, the mind, the senses and the organs of sense, the subtle principle of the elements, and the elements themselves. As these combine and recombine in various ways, all beings attain to existence.

Among these there are Sthāvara, or stationary beings, such as herbs, shrubs, creepers and plants. They have unmanifested consciousness. In them sense of touch alone has evolved.

Then there are the brute species, the animals, in which the sense of smell is highly developed.

Next comes man.

Lastly, there are the Devas, the Pitris the Gandharvas, and the Kinnaras. These are gods, demigods, angels, and spirits.

All things whatsoever, O Vidura, were created by Brahmā.

Thus it was that Creation came to pass :

While the world was yet submerged beneath the ocean, God lay brooding on Ananta, king of the serpents, as Ananta floated upon the waters. God was resting, with eyes closed, but his consciousness was fully awake. He was completely merged in the bliss of his own Self.

As the time of creation drew nigh, God felt a stir within his being, and there issued forth from the centre of his person a full-blown Lotus. Its luminosity was dazzling, and the whole ocean was lighted by its splendour.

Within this Lotus were all the materials for creation. God himself was absorbed within it, and became its innermost being.

Immediately Brahmā came forth from the Lotus, and, seating himself upon it, turned his head in all directions to see whether any other beings were present. Hence he is called the four-faced Brahmā.

Brahmā did not recognize himself, and had no recollection of his previous creations. Thereupon he became restless, and a desire for knowledge rose within his heart. Looking about him and seeing in the external world no hope for the fulfilment of his desires, he sought in meditation for the knowledge which he realized must be within himself, and at last he found the Truth, and God himself, within his own heart. He then saw God everywhere, and felt blest indeed.

Then God spoke to him, saying :

" O Brahmā, I command thee : again create the world, as thou hast often done in times past. To create is to thee not new. Whatsoever is to be created is already within me, as thou well knowest. Creation is only the projection into form of that which already exists."

During this time a strong wind had arisen, and was lashing the water into fury. So, with the knowledge and power which he had acquired through the practice of Tapas, Brahmā withdrew into himself the wind and all the waters of the sea. Then finding himself floating in the ether, still seated upon the Lotus, he re-entered the heart of the Lotus, and dividing it into three sections created the three spheres—heaven, earth and sky.

Brahmā also gave to the world the four Vedas : namely, the Rik, the Sāma, the Yajur, and the Atharva.

Brahmā is the personification of what the philosophers call the Sphota, the word OM. He is also called the first-born of God.

Brahmā's first human creations were saints, who, immediately upon being created, fell into deep meditation finding no interest in the things of the world. Thus, through them, Brahmā saw no possibility of propagation of the human species. While he was meditating upon what course he should pursue, his own form divided itself ; one half became man and the other half became woman.

The man was called Manu, and the woman Śatarūpā ; and from them have sprung all mankind.

CHAPTER III

THE BIRTH OF KAPILA

Vidura :

GLADLY would I hear further concerning Manu and Śatarūpā ; pray tell me more.

Maitreya :

In the course of time, two sons and three daughters were born to Manu and Śatarūpā. The sons were Priyavrata and Uttānapāda. The three daughters were Ākūti, Devahūti, and Prāsūti. I will relate to you the stories of some of these children of Manu. First, let me tell you about Devahūti, for to her was born the renowned sage and philosopher Kapila.

Devahūṭi had grown to be a beautiful young girl, and her parents were anxious that she should find a suitable husband. They travelled through various countries and at last met a young man of exceeding charm, very learned and a great saint. His name was Kardama, and it was said that he was born of the heart of Brahmā. As soon as Devahūti met him, she loved him, to the great joy of her parents Manu and Śatarūpā. Kardama on his part was charmed by the beauty of the girl, and it was not long before Manu gave him his beloved daughter in marriage and returned to his own kingdom.

Through the practice of Tapas, Kardama had learned to exercise great self-control. This practice he taught his wife, and in worship and meditation they lived together for some time without conjugal relations. But Devahūti, though happy in the service of her beloved husband, desired to have children. Kardama therefore yielded to the wish of his wife, and she was made happy by the birth of several beautiful daughters. But she wished also for a son. In time this wish, too, was fulfilled, and Kapila was born. Kapila was amazingly beautiful, lotus-eyed and golden-haired. He was born with divine powers and endowed with divine wisdom and a knowledge of all the Scriptures.

Now that Kardama had fulfilled his duty to his wife, he wished to retire and devote the remainder of his life to the contemplation of God. And so, renouncing the world, he took to the life of monk. Soon, by unswerving devotion, he realized Brahman, the impersonal Truth, and rising above physical consciousness looked with an equal eye upon happiness and misery, heat and cold, success and failure. When he attained absolute poise, no longer did waves of desire arise to disturb the calmness of his mind. And finally his heart was united with God ; he became one with him and saw all beings in the divine Self, and the divine Self in all beings.

Thus it was that Kardama, having realized this highest unity, achieved absolute freedom.

CHAPTER IV

KAPILA'S TEACHINGS CONCERNING DIVINE LOVE

Maitreya : (*continuing*)

DEVAHUTI had good reason to be proud of her beloved son Kapila. He was born a free soul and a natural teacher of mankind, and he became the founder of the school of Sānkhya Philosophy.[1] She herself had an innate yearning for the highest knowledge, and it was naturally her privilege to discuss philosophy and religion with him. One day she said to him :

---

[1] The *Sānkhya* Philosophy as given here and in the subsequent chapters by the author of the Śrimad Bhāgavatam, differs in some details, but not in spirit, from the Sānkhya Philosophy of Kapila.

My son, you are very dear to me. Will you not tell me of that knowledge through which I may find freedom from the bondage of the world? Since taking on the duties of family life, I have become more and more attached to the world. In my youth I learned much from your beloved father, Kardama; now in my old age would I gladly learn wisdom of his son.

Kapila:

O Mother, one finds complete cessation of misery by following the Yoga that teaches unity with the divine Self. This Yoga brings the highest good to humanity. I taught it to the saints of yore in my previous incarnations, and I will now teach it to you.

Mind alone is the cause of the bondage or freedom of the soul. By the attachment of the mind to the world we become bound; by the devotion of the mind to God we become free.

Give up all ideas of "me" and "mine," for thus alone is the heart purified, and so freed from lust, greed, and delusion. In a pure heart are manifested knowledge and love; and the true Self, which is divine, self-luminous, pure and free, is realized.

The wise truly say that attachment to the things of the world is the cause of bondage and suffering. Yet attachment brings freedom when directed toward devout men. These are they who are self-controlled, forbearing, loving, and friendly to all. They dwell in the consciousness of God ; their hearts are united with God. No sorrow or grief, therefore, can agitate their minds or disturb their equilibrium. They are free from all attachment.

All who associate with such men, and love them, become pure. By living in a holy atmosphere, by hearing the praises of the Lord daily, they develop faith in God and reverence for him. Finally, they take delight in the thought of him, and find love for him filling their hearts. Then assuredly they meditate upon him and become entirely devoted to him.

When a man has had such an experience, there is no longer any attraction for him in the pleasures of senses. He is freed from the meshes of ignorance, his heart becomes illumined, and, even in this earthly life, he realizes the kingdom of heaven.

Devahūti :

Tell me how I may love God. Teach me that love which would easily bring freedom. Also tell me about the Yoga of meditation.

Kapila :

Our senses, O Mother, draw us to things because we love the world. If we direct our love toward God we find divine knowledge and absolute freedom. But there are souls who find such great joy in love and in the service of the Lord that they have no concern for their own salvation. Even so, divine love ultimately brings freedom to them also.

Those who love God as dearly as themselves ; those who have affection for him as for their children ; those who trust him as their beloved companion, and reverence him as the teacher of all teachers, those who love him as their dear friend, and worship him as God—theirs is eternal life.

Blessed indeed are they that steadfastly devote themselves to the worship of God, for they shall attain to absolute freedom.[1]

I am God, the Lord of the universe. I am the Self in all beings. I am fearless. I free all from the fears of the world. From fear of me the wind blows ; from fear of me the sun sheds light and heat, and the clouds yield rain ; and from fear of me fire burns. The Yogis

---

[1] In the following paragraph Kapila continues to speak, but in so doing identifies himself with his inner Self, or God.

worship and serve me, who am fearless. They love me and meditate on me in order to realize the highest good. When the heart becomes calm, and the mind becomes united in me through love, then is attained the supreme good.

CHAPTER V

THE CAUSE OF MISERY AND THE WAY TO FREEDOM

Kapila : (*continuing*)

Now, O Mother, I will tell you of that Truth, knowing which man becomes free from the meshes of ignorance.

The light of the inner consciousness which exists as the Self of man is also known as the Purusha. The Purusha is self-luminous, without beginning and without end, and entirely separate from Prakriti. The universe of name and form is an outcome of Prakriti, energized by her nearness to the Purusha. The Purusha, identifying himself with Prakriti—that is, with the non-Self—becomes deluded in Avidyā and his consciousness becomes finite. The Purusha is the eternal witness, always free, and never the performer of actions. All actions proceed from the Guṇas of Prakriti, but because of super-imposition and identification, Purusha thinks himself their performer, though in reality he is blissful and free. He seems bound by Karmas, and remains subject to birth and death, and is either happy or sorrowful.

Devahūti :

I understand that Prakriti is the cause of this universe—subtle and gross. But, tell me, what is Prakriti ?

Kapila :

Prakriti is that which, though undifferentiated has within itself the cause of all differentiation. Prakriti consists of three Guṇas—Sattva, Rajas, and Tamas. When these Guṇas are in equilibrium, in perfect balance, the state is known as Prakriti, or nature quiet and formless. When the balance of the Guṇas is disturbed, then is the universe projected.

The Purusha is without form, without attributes, changeless ; therefore he cannot be the performer of actions. As the sun, though reflected in water, is not affected by the attributes of water, so the Purusha, though living in the body, is not affected by the attributes of the Guṇas of Prakriti. But because, through ignorance, the Purusha identifies himself with the Guṇas, he seems to be happy or sorrowful and thinks himself the performer of actions. Hence his bondage to Karma, which subjects him to birth and death in this world, with the result that he is born as beast, man, angel, or god.

As the mind is allowed to cling to the world and the objects of the world, attachment grows, and there comes delusion. He who desires to rise above the world must learn self-control by the practice of non-attachment.

Follow the path of the Yoga of meditation. Be steadfastly devoted to God, and with a concentrated mind dwell in the thought of God.

Learn to look with an equal eye upon all beings ; shun all hatred and enmity ; and with a cheerful heart surrender yourself to the Feet of the Lord.

Be content, no matter what your lot ;
In eating, drinking and recreation, be moderate ;
Walk in the paths of solitude ; seek peace within your heart ;
Be a friend to all, make no complaint of their faults,
With sympathy minister to their suffering :

Make ready thus to receive that knowledge
  which reveals the Truth.
So shall you free yourself from the meshes of
  ignorance;
So shall you free yourself from the bondage
  of earthly consciousness:
Then shall you realize the Self—
The infinite and holy Purusha, divinely free.

As a man while sleeping may dream unhappy dreams, but when waking, though he remember them, is not deluded by them, so, when man recognizes the Self within, realizes its divinity, and delights in its glory, he is no longer deluded by Prakirti. He has conquered life and death—he knows the bliss of heaven. Even the Yoga powers can no longer tempt him, for he has control over them. On earth he lives a free soul, and when at last death claims his body, he attains that divine freedom than which there is no greater joy.

CHAPTER VI

THE YOGA OF MEDITATION

Kapila: (*continuing*)

I WILL now explain to you the Yoga of meditation.

The first step to this Yoga is observance of the moral precepts, which must be obeyed by all. These are :

Do your duties faithfully, no matter how lowly your condition in life. Surrender the fruits of your actions to God. Seek the society of the holy and do service to them. Above all, acquire an eager thirst for righteousness, truth and freedom.

Practise moderation in your appetites. Do injury to no creature.

Swerve not from the truth. Covet not the wealth of another.

Accept only enough for your daily needs.

Practise self-control and self-denial, that you may lead a pure, continent life. Before all else, be clean and pure in soul, mind, and body.

And finally, study the Scriptures with diligence.

To practise meditation one should select a secluded place and use it for that purpose only. When one is seated he must hold the body erect, but not tense. Then he must practise control of the Prāṇa, with the help of breathing exercises. The mind must then be gathered into itself and not permitted to dwell on external objects.

Next, the mind must be fixed on one of the centres of consciousness within the body. This final act is known as the practise of concentration.

Thus prepared, one should meditate on the divine attributes.

Through these practices will come remarkable spiritual growth. By the practice of Prāṇāyāmā you may acquire physical health. As you practise Pratyāhāra you will cease to be attached to external objects. Practice of concentration will bring you purity of heart, and meditation will enable you to unite yourself with the Divine.

Thus, when your mind and heart become calm and pure, you will learn to dwell in the consciousness of God. Then will you find divine love.

Devahūti :

Tell me more about the religion of love, for it is not possible to practise the Yoga of meditation without love for God.

Kapila :

Love is divine. But love is expressed differently and in different degrees according to the evolution of the individual human soul.

There are people who still have hatred, jealousy, anger and pride in their hearts. To such, God is above, beyond and apart. They also may love God, but their love is selfish. This love is Tāmasika.

That, too, is a low form of love by which people love and worship God as a separate being, and pray to him for the fulfilment of their material desires. Such love is known as Rājasika love.

But the love which seeks God for the sake of love alone and by means of which we offer ourselves whole-heartedly to him—this love we call Sāttvika love.

But when the love, the lover, and the beloved have become one, when we see God and love him as the innermost Self in all beings, and when there is a continuous current of love flowing in the heart, then is it that we realize divine love.

When such divine love fills the heart, we transcend the three Guṇas and become united with Brahman.

In order that the heart may be purified and divine love may increase, one should obey the following precepts :

Perform the duties of life, but work without thought of reward. Work must be turned into worship.

Offer worship to God regularly. Chant his name. Sing his praises and dwell more and more in the thought of him.

Learn to see God in all beings. Revere the great sages. Be kindly to the poor and the destitute, and friendly to all.

Thus may one attain the kingdom of heaven.

God dwells as the innermost Self in the hearts of all beings and all things, although he is not manifest in the same degree in all. He is most manifest in the pure in heart, and in him who has realized the unity that is in the midst of diversity.

I am the Self in all beings.[1] I dwell in the hearts of all. Where else shall one worship me but in all beings? Knowing me as the Self in all beings, love all, and live in the service of all.

Devahūti followed so faithfully the teachings of her beloved son that she soon found God manifest within her own heart and in the hearts of all beings.

Kapila after a time took leave of his mother, and renouncing all earthly ties journeyed north into the Himālayas. It is said that he still lives in Yoga, completely absorbed in Samādhi for the good of all mankind.

---

[1] Again Kapila suddenly identifies himself with God.

BOOK FOURTH

THE ARGUMENT

SUTA continues to relate, after Śuka, the *Bhāgavatam*. In the part here included Maittreya, still addressing Vidura, goes on with an account of the earliest men and women.

CHAPTER I

THE STORY OF DHRUVA

KING Uttānapāda was the son of Manu, the first man born of Brahmā. Dhruva was the son of King Uttānapāda and of Sunīti, his first wife. The second wife of the king was Suruchi, whom he loved deeply but feared because of her unreasonable jealousy.

One day King Uttānapāda and Suruchi were sitting together, playing with their little son Uttama. Tempted by the merriment, Dhruva, who was five years old at this time, approached and asked his father's permission to join in the play, but the king paid no attention to the plea of his older son. This attitude of indifference pleased Suruchi, who had no love for her stepson. Turning to Dhruva she said, "That you are the king's son, I do not doubt. But no son of the king is worthy to aspire to the throne unless he is born of me. If, therefore, you aspire to this kingdom, practise austerities throughout this life and pray that you may be worthy to be born of me in your next life."

Dhruva made no reply to Suruchi but turned to his father for some word of comfort. Finding no response, he burst into tears and ran to his mother.

Sunīti's heart smote her when she saw her son weeping so bitterly. She took him in her arms, kissed away his tears, and soothed him with gentle whispers. When his sobs subsided and he was calm, she said :

" O my son, let not the words of your stepmother affect you so deeply. Feel sorrow for her rather than anger. You know that through the law of Karma her deeds will sometime return to her again. Remember only the one great truth she told you. It is indeed true that through prayer and the practice of Tapas and the grace of God everything is possible. God, my son, is our only refuge and comfort."

" Tell me, Mother, who is God and where shall I find him ? " asked Dhruva.

" He is said to be ' lotus-eyed,' " answered Sunīti. " He alone can wipe out all miseries and fulfil all desires. Those who take refuge in him with undivided heart and soul receive his grace ; but he is not easily attainable. The Yogis find him within their hearts through whole-souled devotion."

Dhruva listened attentively to the words of his mother and determined in his heart to be a Yogi. He would find God. But who could teach him the Yoga practices ?

It is said that the light is within our hearts, covered with darkness, and that it can be revealed only by a soul who has uncovered his own light. Such a soul is the real teacher. Dhruva went forth in search of someone qualified to teach him how to find God, the lotus-eyed.

Nārada, the great sage, while communing with God, felt the soul's thirst in the simple young boy Dhruva. He knew that the lad was sincerely yearning for God and needed help. Nārada therefore went out to meet Dhruva that he might teach him the path to God.

When he had found the boy, he blessed him. At first he made as if to dissuade him from the path. To test his earnestness, Nārada said :

" My boy, you are very young. You should enjoy life and the pleasures of the world. The path of God is hard to follow. The Yogis struggle in the path, forsaking all the pleasures of life for many, many years, and even for many lives, before they find him. So why not give up this almost vain search? Return to your home and live a good life. Delight in association with great men. Be kind and sympathetic to all. Follow this simple teaching, and you will be happy. Then, when old age comes, devote yourself to meditation."

Dhruva expressed his gratitude to the kindly sage, but added humbly:

"O most revered sir, I desire the highest attainment, the realization of the supreme goal of life—I wish to find God. Pray teach me the path."

Nārada replied:

"My child, you are rightly determined. Blessed indeed are those who devote themselves to the worship of God. All the desires of their heart shall be fulfilled, and they shall attain the highest freedom."

Nārada then initiated him into the sacred path of Yoga. He taught him Prāṇāyāma, consisting of three parts: exhaling, inhaling, and holding the breath. He pointed out how this practice of breathing would help to bring control over the Prāṇa and the senses; and how the mind, when free from restlessness, would become fit for the practice of meditation.

When Dhruva had mastered this practice, Nārada taught him how to meditate.

Dhruva's chosen ideal of God was Viṣṇu, or Vāsudeva.

Nārada therefore taught Dhurva how to meditate upon Viṣṇu within the sanctuary of his heart. "Feel yourself in his loving presence," he said. "Feel his love, his protection, and his guidance." He then gave him the sacred Mantram "OM, namo Bhagavate Vāsudevāya" (the name of the Lord who was Dhruva's chosen ideal of the God of Love), saying :

"Repeat this name mentally and offer worship and prayer to the Lord with this Mantram. See Vāsudeva within your own heart ; see him everywhere and in all beings. Steadfastly devote yourself to the worship of God, and you will know the Truth even in this life."

Nārada then advised Dhruva to go to Madhuvana, a retreat on the bank of the sacred Yamuna, to practise meditation in that secluded and sacred atmosphere where God is most manifest. Prince Dhruva prostrated himself at the feet of his master and went to Madhuvana to practise Tapas.

Nārada, glad at heart, went to visit King Uttānapāda, who received him with due reverence. Finding the king sad, Nārada asked the reason for his grief. The king replied :

"O revered master, my heart is torn with anxiety and yearning for my son Dhruva. To please my wife, I sent him away from me, unloved and very unhappy. Now, I know not where he is, and my heart is sorrowful. Oh, surely I am the most cruel and the most deluded of kings and fathers."

Touched by his grief, Nārada comforted him thus:

"O king, despair not. Your son is alive and well. He is under divine protection, and no harm will befall him. His fame will spread far and wide, and when at last he returns to you, you will share the glory of his renown."

These words from the lips of the holy man brought calmness to the heart of the troubled king.

Now Dhruva was at Madhuvana, practising Tapas very earnestly. During the first days he felt a restlessness of spirit; but soon he gained control over his mind and found joy in meditation. He made such progress that by the fifth month he had risen above all physical consciousness. He was unaware of the surrounding world; his mind was absorbed in the thought of Brahman.

With the sixth month he went still deeper into meditation. Veil after veil of ignorance and darkness was lifted. He beheld the divine light, the divine being, his chosen ideal Vāsudeva-smiling, benign-within the shrine of his heart. The experience was so real, the divine presence so vivid, that the world of sense vanished into nothingness. Dhruva's blessedness was inexpressible—to him the radiant immanence of God was all.

But this Samādhi did not last. He soon awakened, and as he opened his eyes he saw before him Vāsudeva—the same face of God that he had seen within his heart. The whole universe was lighted by his presence. Dhruva's heart melted in love, and from the fullness of his joy he sang the praises of the Lord:

"O thou great friend of the poor and the destitute,
Thou art the refuge of all;
Thou dost deliver us from the round of birth and death
May I ever love thee! May I ever be one in that blessed company of the pure who loved thee!
Thou art the infinite Brahman,
Unchangeable, unequalled, without beginning and without end,
Thy form is bliss;
Thou art the supreme goal;
I take refuge in Thee."

Then the Lord spoke unto him:

"I know thy heart, my child. Thou didst desire to be a king. Know that thou shalt rule thy father's kingdom for many years. After thy allotted time of life on earth, thou shalt go to that place in heaven called the celestial sphere, where the gods and angels and stars circle round and round, singing my praises and glory. Thou shalt be the centre of that sphere, and thou shalt be known as the Dhruva Nakshatra, the polar star."

Thus saying, the Lord disappeared from his vision.

Dhruva felt sad at heart. He had once desired the love of his father, and his rights as heir to his father's kingdom, but now he found how trivial such things were, when compared with spiritual bliss. He realized that he had been like one who dug a well to satisfy his thirst while living on the bank of a river. He no longer felt any other desire than to love and serve God.

He calmed himself, however, and obeying the will of the Lord journeyed back to his father's kingdom.

When King Uttānapāda learned that his son Dhruva was returning he called together his wife, their son Uttama, Sunīti, the mother of Dhruva, and numerous attendants. Then, with many gorgeously decorated carriages and amid great pomp and ceremony, he set out to meet him.

As soon as he saw Dhruva approaching, the king ran to him and embraced him tenderly. Dhruva prostrated himself at his father's feet; then he bowed down to his stepmother Suruchi, who embraced him, and kissing him affectionately, said:

"May you live long, my child. I beg you to forgive me; one who is dear to God is dear to all beings. No enmity or hatred can endure before him. I am proud and blessed to call you my child."

Dhruva now affectionately embraced his young brother Uttama. Then he prostrated himself at the feet of his mother, who with an overwhelming happiness flooding her heart, raised him up.

There was great rejoicing in the city as Dhruva passed through it on his way to the palace.

When Dhruva came of age King Uttānapāda placed him on the throne; and, with the permission of his beloved subjects, retired into solitude to spend the remainder of his life in the contemplation of God.

Now it happened that one day while Dhruva's young brother Uttama was out hunting, he was slain by a Yakṣa, a demigod.

When Dhruva heard of this he became angry and declared war against the Yakṣas and their chief, Kubera, the god of wealth and the regent of the north. While the war was still raging and many Yakṣas were being slain, Manu, Dhruva's grandfather, came with other saints and requested Dhruva to desist from fighting and from killing the innocent Yakṣas. Manu spoke to him thus :

" Why do you fight in this manner ? Because of your grief for the loss of your brother, you have lost mastery over your passions, and have been deluded. Why do you grieve for one who is not really dead ? Bodies have a beginning and an end, but the soul is immortal.

" You attained knowledge and gained power through your devotion to God ; yet some ignorance remains in you, for you still see difference, and not the unity that pervades all things. Now must you therefore seek the highest truth, so that you may find one God, the divine Self, in all beings and in all things, and thus be forever free from all delusion."

As Manu reminded him of this truth, Dhruva at once realized his great weakness, and immediately all his anger left him. He ceased warring against the Yakṣas, and his heart was again filled with love for all.

When Kubera, the chief of the Yakṣas, heard of Dhruva's decision, he appeared before him and offered to be his friend. Now Kubera had the power to fulfil the desires of men. He therefore offered to Dhruva any boon that he might choose.

Dhruva replied :

" If it please thee to fulfil the desire of my heart, grant me this one boon—that I may always remember the Lord ; for only by living continuously in the consciousness of God can a man become free from the delusions of the world."

Kubera at once granted this request and then disappeared.

After a peaceful reign of a few years, Dhruva renounced the throne in favour of his son, Utkala, and wishing to regain that sublime experience of his youth wherein he had known himself indissolubly united with God, he went away to the sacred retreat of Badarika in the Himālayas. There, in daily solitude and meditation, he dwelt with God. There he again lost the consciousness of this manifold and finite universe in a vivid awareness of the divine unity and immensity. Finally, the consciousness of his own personal, finite ego was lost, and there remained only the unitary consciousness in which the " I " and God become one. He was aware only of the one absolute existence, absolute knowledge, and absolute bliss. At last he knew himself to be one with the God of Love.

When Dhruva regained his normal consciousness, he knew that the time was approaching for giving up his physical body, the garment of his soul. Suddenly he saw in a vision a luminous chariot coming down from heaven to carry him away. Everything about him, was lighted by its radiance. Two celestial beings, attendants of Lord Viṣṇu, descended from the chariot and addressed Dhruva, saying :

" We have been sent by Lord Viṣṇu to take you to his abode."

Dhruva recognized them as the attendants of God and bowed down to them. He then chanted the name of the Lord Viṣṇu and putting aside his earthly form, mounted the chariot. As the chariot ascended, he heard singing and rejoicing all around him.

Dhruva was carried to the celestial sphere, and, as promised by the Lord, he became the polar star, the guide of all mankind in every age.[1]

---

[1] To this day Hindus call the polar star Dhruva Nakṣatra.

CHAPTER II

UTKALA, SON OF DHRUVA

UTKALA, the son of Dhruva, was a great saint. He had been born with natural poise, and calmness, and knowledge of God.

The responsibility of ruling the earth imposed upon him by his father soon became burdensome to him, and he forthwith abdicated the throne in favour of his younger brother, Vatsara, who ruled the earth for many years.

Utkala chose the life of renunciation and solitude, realizing that the divine Self exists in all human beings, and that all beings exist in the divine Self. His heart found itself united with all things. All his worldly desires were burned in the fire of knowledge. He was filled with great love for God, and enjoyed peace ineffable. He lived in the consciousness of God during his entire life, aware of nothing but the divine Ātman, and spent his days teaching words of wisdom and singing the praises of the Lord.

CHAPTER III

KING PRITHU

KING PRITHU, a descendant of Dhruva, was a great man and a noble king.

While the people of his court were still enjoying the festivities of the day of his coronation, news came to him of a terrible famine which was raging over the land. Thousands of people were dying of hunger. Even as the messengers spoke, multitudes began to flock to the palace crying for food.

The king realized at once how great was the calamity that had come upon him. He knew that the earth was not sufficiently productive, and wondered sadly what could be done to relieve the condition of his people. While he was meditating on the problem, Mother Earth herself, in the form of a cow, appeared before him.

She gave the king to understand that she was able and willing to yield all that was necessary for man, but that man must exert himself to obtain it. She could produce diverse foods, she said, and all necessities, suited to all peoples and to every climate.

King Prithu therefore called some of his subjects to him and with care and patience explained to them all that Mother Earth had told him. Later, through the efforts of the king and his subjects, Mother Earth yielded corn, herbs, plants, and trees, in quantities sufficient to satisfy the physical needs of mankind. To the sages she yielded food for the spirit —

namely, the Vedas. To the Devas she yielded immortality, mental vigour, power of the senses, and physical strength. To the Rākshasas she yielded intoxicating drinks. From her the Gandharva received beauty and sweetness, the Siddhas Yogic powers, and the Vidyādharas knowledge. In this manner did Mother Earth fulfil the desires of all her children.

Under the benign rule of King Prithu, forts, cities, towns, villages, homes, and factories were built, and these brought comfort and protection to his subjects, who became happy and prosperous. There was no more want or famine during his long reign.

When peace and happiness had been restored, King Prithu invited all the people of the earth and the gods of the heaven to join him in a magnificent sacrificial rite. Lord Viṣṇu came down from his highest abode in response to the king's prayer. After blessing his votary, Lord Viṣṇu taught him these truths :

" The wise man neither hates nor injures anyone. He sees the one divine Self in all. Neither does he become attached to the body, for he knows that the bondage of Karma clings to him who ignorantly identifies himself with it. When one frees himself from attachment to the body, he will have no more attachment to the world.

" The Ātman, or divine Self, is separate from the body. This Ātman is One without a second, pure, self-luminous, without attributes, free, all-pervading. He is the eternal witness. Blessed is he who knows this Ātman, for though an embodied being he shall be free from the changes and qualities pertaining to the body. He alone is ever united with me.

" He who, being desireless, worships me, with his heart and mind absorbed in me, soon finds joy. His heart, finding delight in me, becomes free from attachment to the Guṇas. He becomes the seer of Truth, and realizes abiding peace and freedom in me.

" The Ātman is ever free. Those who know the Ātman as the ruler of the body, senses, mind, and intellect, become fearless, and are free from all bondage. They know that the body alone is subject to birth and death, and that the Ātman is ever free and immortal. No grief can overcome them, for they are united with me in love.

" O king, thou art wise. Be not deluded by either happiness or misery. Look with an equal eye upon all beings, and rule this kingdom with your senses and mind under perfect control.

"I am not easily attainable by sacrificial rites or ceremonies, nor by austerities, but I reveal myself unto those who see me in all beings and all beings in me."

King Prithu prostrated himself at the feet of the Lord of Love, and prayed :

"O Lord of my heart,

"May I always hear thy praise and sing thy glory, and my heart be ever filled with love for thee. This is my only prayer."

Lord Viṣṇu accepted the worship of his devotee and then disappeared. But he dwelt forever in the heart of King Prithu.

The king then taught his subjects how to worship God sincerely, with their hearts and minds absorbed in meditation upon him. He taught them that even the desire to serve him freed man from impurities accumulated during many lives, and that blessed indeed was the man who surrendered himself to the Lotus Feet of the Lord, for he should be free from all impurities and all attachment, should have knowledge of Truth, and should conquer death. Thus the king taught his subjects how to attain the kingdom of heaven.

One day, while his subjects from the fullness of their hearts were praising their beloved king, there appeared before him four great Rishis, headed by Sanatkumāra. Their forms were luminous, and their faces shone like those of the knowers of Brahman.

The king welcomed them reverently, and with a gladdened heart spoke to them thus :

" O revered saints, ye are born of Brahmā, and are denizens of the Jana Loka. It is a great blessing to meet you on earth. What a sweetness and joy to be associated with you ! You see no diversity, but only unity. I know you to be the friends of mankind. Tell us, I pray you, what would be of the greatest good to humanity ? "

Sanatkumāra, the eldest of the Riṣis, replied :

" O king, it is a pleasure to meet thee and talk to thee ; for thou takest delight in hearing of God. All impurities are washed away from the hearts of those who take delight in the Word of God.

" The following things have been ascertained and declared by all the Scriptures of the world to be of the greatest good to mankind :

" First, to delight in the Self, which is one with God, or to love God ; and secondly to be without attachment to anything else in the universe.

" This true love and non-attachment must be developed gradually by these means :

" By faith and reverence.

" By inquiry into the Truth.

" By devotion to spiritual practices.

" By worshipping the great souls who have realized the Truth.

" By taking delight in the Word of God.

" By shunning the association of the worldly.

" By learning to love solitude.

" By injuring no creature and by truthfulness.

" By studying the Scriptures.

" By control of the senses.

" By overcoming the passions.

" By not speaking against other religions.

" By patiently bearing the opposites of life, such as pleasure and pain, success and failure.

" By singing the praises and glory of God.

" Thus will arise love for God and non-attachment to the world.

" When love is firmly established in his heart, a man becomes master of himself and a teacher of humanity. He is born anew ; his ego is consumed in the fire of knowledge.

" The ego is the cause of ignorance. When the ego is subdued, the spiritual consciousness shines forth in all its glory. One realizes the divine Self. The manifold universe, with all its pleasure and pain, vanishes like a dream. There remains the unitary blissful consciousness, the Ātman.

"Thinking of objects attracts the senses to them. The senses being attracted, the mind becomes attached. When this attachment grows in the mind, man loses all power of discrimination. Losing the power of discrimination, he becomes deluded. Being deluded, he loses all memory. All memory being lost, there is lost the knowledge of the Ātman, the divine Self. The loss of this knowledge is called by the wise 'losing one's own Self.' What greater calamity can there be than to lose one's own Self? Everything is dear to us because of the Self. When the Self is lost, what remains?

"Lustful thoughts and the desire for the things of the world—these are the greatest enemies of knowledge and to the unfoldment of divinity. Such thoughts make man dull and ignorant. Therefore should a man shun them.

"O king, know the God of Love alone; know Him who is to be directly realized and who dwelleth in the hearts of all beings and things. He alone abideth forever. All else is transitory. He can be directly perceived. He is expressed in and through even the minutest cells. He is all-pervading. He is the truth. He is pure and ever free. May I take refuge in Him!

" As on a dark night one sees a rope as a snake, so, because of ignorance, does one see the one absolute existence as this manifold universe. But, as when the light comes, the snake vanishes, so when the light of knowledge dawns, the manifold universe vanishes and there remains the Sachchidānanda—absolute existence, absolute knowledge, and absolute bliss.

" Blessed indeed are they who meditate on the Lotus Feet of the God of Love, for they shall be free from all impurities and from bondage of the heart.

" Worship him alone. Six passions there are—lust, anger, greed, pride, delusion and jealousy—which are like ferocious sharks in the ocean of the world. Accept Him as thy pilot, and cross the ocean with ease, and without fear."

Receiving these teachings from Sanatkumāra, the king devoted himself to contemplation of the divine Self. As his power of concentration grew, he felt a greater fullness of life within. Though he lived in the world, he remained perfectly unattached ; for he was free from ego, his heart was pure, and the objects of the world and worldly enjoyments could not draw his senses and mind in their direction.

After some years had passed, he abdicated the throne in favour of his son Vijitāśva, and retired into the solitude of the forest life. There he practised many austerities and lived a life of meditation. Soon his mind, free from all worldly thoughts, became deeply absorbed in God, and he realized his unity with Brahman. All doubts vanished. The knots of his heart were loosed.[1]

Knowing that death was approaching, he sat in meditation and let his body dissolve into the elements of which it was composed, and he himself, free from all adjuncts, attained Brahman.

CHAPTER IV

THE CITY OF PURANJANA

In due course Prāchīnabarhis, son of Vijitāśva, became the ruler of the earth. He was a good king, but he had forgotten spiritual truths and was deeply attached to the world. One day the great sage Nārada, who loved the king and felt sorry for him, approached him in the hope that he might bring him out of the deep

---

[1] Literally rendered. Equivalent to : " His heart was released from bondage to the world."

mire of ignorance and teach him the knowledge of God.

" O king," said the sage, " learn to follow the way of good and not the way of pleasure. What do you really hope to gain in life? Complete cessation of miseries and the attainment of eternal happiness are the supreme good and the highest ideals to realize, but your worldliness will not bring you to the realization of them."

To this Prāchīnabarhis replied :

" O thou holy one, my heart is so drawn to things of this world, my intelligence is so covered with ignorance, that I do not know the way of freedom. Pray teach me that knowledge which will free me from worldliness, that I may attain the supreme good."

" I will tell you a story," began Narada, " which illustrates, in allegory, what I wish to teach.

" There lived a well-known king, named Puranjana. He had an intimate friend, but none knew his name or his occupation.

" Puranjana roamed all over the earth hoping to find a suitable place to live. But he met only with disappointment. He thought to himself, ' I have seen many cities, but none appears good to me. I want to live in one where all my desires may be satisfied, but none of these would be sufficient for the purpose.'

"At last he came to a city in Bhāratavarsha, south of the Himālayas. This magnificent city, with its nine gates, its stately palaces, its beautiful gardens, and crystal lakes, appeared to have all the advantages he had been seeking. He felt that his wanderings were over, for here all his desires could be gratified.

"Then, one day soon after, Puranjana saw a beautiful young girl, with her attendants, walking in a garden. Their paths met, they fell in love, and within a short time they were married. They continued to live in the city of nine gates, and it was by passing through these gates that Puranjana found he could indulge his many desires, although, strange to say, he never found a real satisfaction in so doing. He loved his wife deeply, and was happy only when in her presence. He made her wishes his, and when she wept, he wept, when she smiled, he smiled. Thus slavishly responsive to her every whim and mood, he was on the way to losing the last vestige of his independence.

"For many years he stayed on in that beautiful city, gratifying his every desire but never obtaining any lasting pleasure or comfort from his way of life.

" Now it happened that while King Puranjana, immersed in pleasures, was forgetful of everything else, a mighty general attacked the city where he dwelt. This general possessed a certain magical charm by means of which he had the power to work great havoc. So it was that now he demolished the beautiful city of nine gates. Puranjana himself could not escape. He found himself bereft of everything, even of that last stronghold of consciousness, his memory. He forgot well-nigh all—his past, his kingship, his magnificent city. One memory alone was left : the thought of his beautiful wife. This thought possessed his mind with such intensity that he did not notice his loss of memory for the rest of the world. His whole nature became obsessed by her image, and like a madman who, losing his own identity becomes the being whose image possesses him, so Puranjana found himself transformed into a lovely young girl like his wife.

" The young girl he had now become forgot her previous identity to such an extent that when she met with King Malayadhvaja, she fell in love with him and married him. When in the course of time the king passed away, and she was left alone, lamenting his death and her bereavement, an unknown Brahmin came to her and said :

" 'O my beloved friend, why are you grieving? Do you not know me, your dear friend? Try to remember who and what you are. I have been your friend always, but you neglected me, and forgetting me entirely went away in search of pleasure and enjoyment. You and I are friends, united in eternal bonds. Though you forgot me, I have been with you all the time. You entered into a city of nine gates and became so deeply attached to a woman that you forgot your real Self. Then later you became forgetful of your past and believed yourself to be the wife of this man. You are neither the husband nor the wife. There is no sex in you. You and I are not separate. Know yourself as me. Just as one sees himself as two when reflected in a mirror, so do you appear as you and I, but in reality we are one.' "

Prāchīnabarhis requested Nārada to explain the allegory, and Nārada, assenting, thus went on:

"O king, Puranjana in the story stands for the Purusha, the divine Self. He is called the Puranjana because the divine Self is the manifestor of Pura, or the body. The unknown friend that I have mentioned is Brahman, or God. None knows him, for no deeds or attributes can express or reveal him.

" The Puras, or bodies, are of various kinds. Of these the human body is a suitable instrument for the enjoyment of all desires. This human body is the city with nine gates, such as eyes, ears, nose, etc., through which the divine Self or Puranjana goes out, as it were, to enjoy the objects of sense. The wife is the intellect, united with whom man enjoys the world and worldly goods. In this identifying itself with the intellect or ego, the divine Self forgets its true nature and becomes immersed in ignorance and vanity.

" The great general is all-destructive time, whose charms are disease and death ; Disease and death ultimately destroy this body.

" Man is divine and free and blissful. Being deluded, he superimposes the attributes of the non-Self upon the Self. Hunger and thirst belong to the Prāṇa, lust or desire belongs to the senses and the mind ; but all these are attributed to the Self in man, who is by nature free.

" Forgetful of his true, divine nature, identifying himself with the false ego, man becomes attached to the world and the pleasures of the world. He then is bound by his deeds. As are his deeds, so is his birth.

" The deeds again are of three kinds : Sāttvika, Rājasika, and Tāmasika. A man of

Sāttvika deeds is born in celestial spheres ; a man of Rājasika deeds is born in the struggling world, where there are both happiness and misery ; and a man of Tāmasika deeds has an unhappy birth, in which he becomes completely deluded. Thus are people born, according to their own deeds, in different bodies, as bird or beast, as man or woman, as angel or god. Upward or downward is their course according to their deeds. They either enjoy or suffer as a result of their Karma.

" Life is followed by death. On the whole, life is misery. Just as a man carrying a heavy burden on his head moves it to his shoulder when it becomes unbearable, but yet is not free from the burden itself, so does man carry the burden of misery with him through life. This burden is the burden of Karma. Deeds performed with attachment and selfish desires are done in ignorance ; and man lives in ignorance. It is only when man gains knowledge of the true nature of his divine Self that he becomes free from Karma and free from ignorance. Then he realizes true bliss and eternal life.

" True knowledge and wisdom arise when one loves God and is steadfastly devoted to him. One who has love for God overcomes the world. Such love, indeed, is supreme.

"Hear the Word of God with faith and reverence; study the Scriptures which reveal the truth of God, that love may grow in your heart. Blessed indeed are those who drink the nectar of God's Word, for they are free from selfish pride; free are they from fear, from delusion, and from misery. Blessed indeed are those who meditate on the Lord of Love as the Self within, for they are free from the bondage of ignorance and from enslavement to Karma.

"That deed is a blessed deed which pleases the Lord of Love; and that knowledge is true knowledge which unites our heart with God.

"The Lord is the highest good and supreme refuge of all. He is the dearest of all things dear. He is our very Self. Knowing Him, one has no fear. He who knows this truth, knows Truth indeed; he becomes the teacher of Truth, for he is one with God.

"Life is short: as is the wind, so is mortal life. Every breath of life is a breath of death also.[1] It is folly for us to waste our lives seeking ephemeral pleasures. Seek God, for He alone is our refuge. Be devoted to Him alone, and thus be free from desires."

---

[1] Compare the English poet Thomas Campion ("Sic Transit"): "So every day we live, a day we die."

" Revered master, ' then said Prāchīnabarhis, " what thou hast taught me hast sunk deep into my heart. I will try to follow thy teachings—but I have still a doubt. Pray dispel this doubt for me. It is said, man is what his deeds are. But we do not see that all Karmas produce results immediately. When death overtakes a man, who is there to enjoy or suffer for his deeds? For do not the deeds also die with the passing away of the body?"

" O king," answered Narada, " it is the physical body that dies; the subtle body does not die with death. The impressions of a man's deeds are in the subtle body, and though he leaves his physical body behind with death, his deeds cling to him; and as are his deeds, so is his next birth. He enjoys or suffers in the next life according to his Karma.

" The doer of actions is the ego, which is a product of the identification of the divine Self with the mind or the intellect. Thus the subtle body, or the mind identified with the divine Self, appears as the Jīva, or the individual spirit. All experiences of happiness or misery, fear or delusion, are of the individual spirit. As long as there is this unreal identification, man is bound by his deeds and subject to birth and death. All this bondage is caused by ignorance. With true knowledge comes freedom. The way to this knowledge is to devote oneself to the worship of God and to see Him in all."

Thus taught by Nārada, King Prāchīnabarhis went to Kapilāśrama to practise the way of Truth. There, living in solitude, and devoting himself to meditation on the Lord, he realized Self-knowledge and attained freedom.

CHAPTER V

THE PRACHETAS

KING Prāchīnabarhis had ten sons. They were all called Prachetas and were well known for their virtues. Before they entered into family ties, they lived lives of intense austerity and practised meditation for many years. The Lord of Love was pleased with their steadfast devotion and filled their hearts with gladness and peace, manifesting His glory before them. The Prachetas gave voice to their supreme joy in this song of praise:

"To Thee, O Lord, we bow down!
Thou dost charm away
Life's long dream of sorrow;
With Thy holy name on his lips,
Meditating within the heart

Upon Thy divine attributes,
Man walks Thy blessed path.

" Thou art beyond the reach of the mind ;
Words cannot express Thee ;
The way of the senses is not Thy way.
Blessed are they who know Thy pure blissful Self,
For they shall be free from the bondage of the world.

" We bow down to Thee !
Thou art the Lord of Love,
The Lord of Thy worshippers ;
Thou dost deliver us from all evil.
Blessed are those who know Thee as their very own,
For they shall find peace.

" Thou art the innermost Self of all ;
Thou knowest our heart's desires.
May we realize Thy love !
Thou art limitless and Thy glories boundless,
For Thou art infinite.

" If through bondage to Karma
We go through rounds of birth and death,

May we in every life have the pure joy
Of mingling with Thy devotees :
This we deem the greatest blessing.

" Thy devotees, the free souls, always
speak Thy Word ;
They look with an equal eye upon all ;
Freed from earthly attachments
They live united with Thee
They bless the earth by their living ;
Their lives are a purifying light :
The least association with them
Frees man from the terror of death.

" Thou art indeed the great healer,
The destroyer of worldliness and death,
The giver of eternal life and blessed-
ness.
Who can sing Thy infinite glory ?
Thou art all and everywhere.
We bow down to Thee again and again ! "

Having praised the glory of the infinite Lord, the Prachetas felt a great peace within their hearts.

After many fruitful years of activity in the world, they assumed the lives of Sannyāsins in order to attain the highest knowledge, the knowledge of the one divine Self in all beings and things. Retiring to a place of solitude, they began to practise meditation upon the absolute Brahman. One day as they were seated for meditation, Nārada, the great teacher, approached them. The Prachetas welcomed him with great reverence, beseeching him to teach them the highest Truth, the Truth that would make them free.

So Nārada, uniting his heart with God, began :

" O princes, blessed indeed is that birth, glorious indeed is that act, true indeed is that life, luminous indeed is that mind, and fruitful indeed is that word, which is consecrated to the loving service of God, the Self of the universe.

" Man is born twice : first, he is born of parents ; his next birth is an initiation into the sacred mysteries. But both these births are indeed vain if his life is not dedicated to the loving service of God.

" Vain also are virtuous deeds, and vain is our long life, if we live not in the service of God.

" Love and service—these are the greatest ends of all the Vedas, all austerity, all learning, and all science.

" Useless and futile indeed are Yoga or Sannyāsa, Scriptural study, or virtuous deeds, if one has not love for God in his heart.

"Of all things that exist, the Self is the dearest. The Lord of Love is our very Self. Who then can be dearer than He?

"As when water is poured at the root of a tree, its branches are nourished; as when food is eaten, the senses are strengthened; similarly, when the Lord of the Universe is loved and worshipped, the whole world is filled with rejoicing.

"Therefore, O princes, worship Him within your hearts as one with the Self. He is the Self of all created beings. He is the efficient cause as well as the material cause of the universe. He is the Supreme, the Lord of the universe.

"Love and charity towards all beings, contentment under all circumstances, and control of all the senses and the passions—the practice of these virtues leads to God.

"The Lord is ever manifest in the pure hearts of His devotees."

Thus taught by Nārada, the Prachetas united their hearts and minds with the Lord of Love and realized their unity with Him.

BOOK FIFTH

THE ARGUMENT

THE Sūta continues to relate, after Śuka, the *Bhāgavatam.* Here is given, in the words of the compiler, Vyāsa, the remainder of the story of Manu and Śatarūpā and their direct descendants.

CHAPTER I

PRIYAVRATA, SON OF MANU

O KING Parīkṣit, I have now related to you the story of the descendants of Uttānapāda, the eldest son of Manu. Now I shall tell of the second son of Manu, Priyavrata, and later, of his worthy descendants.

They whose minds drink the nectar of divine bliss, O king, find the highest good and the fullness of life in the contemplation of God and His Word. No temptation can take their minds away from His Lotus Feet.

Priyavrata was a true devotee of God. He realized the spiritual truths through devotion and service to his master, Nārada. He brought his senses under perfect control by untiring service of God. And now when he was ready to renounce the world, and to assume the life of Sannyāsa that he might attain perfect Self-knowledge, he was to find that his father cherished other plans for him. Manu, in fact, wished him to remain in the world, and in accordance with his princely heritage become king of the earth. Priyavrata, however, knowing the vanity of worldly life, refused.

Now Brahmā, the first-born, who knew, through his Yoga power, of Priyavrata's intention, did not approve of the young man's decision. He came down therefore from Satyaloka, his highest heavenly abode, to meet him and reason with him. He found Priyavrata listening to Nārada, who was teaching his beloved disciple the sacred truths. As Brahmā drew nearer, both master and disciple, feeling the presence of a divine being, stood up in reverence and welcomed him.

Brahmā was pleased with their greetings; a heavenly smile lighting his face, he affectionately addressed Priyavrata :

"Learn to surrender thy will to the will of the Lord. His will directs the world : none has power to disobey it. Thy father Manu, thy teacher the great sage Nārada, and I—all of us obey the divine will.

"Human beings are subject to birth and death, grief and delusion, fear and happiness and misery. They do not find any freedom. As a blind man is led either to sunshine or shadow, so are we led by our Karmas to different births—either lower or higher—and we thus experience happiness or misery.

" As a man, after a bad dream, remembers the dream but is not affected by it, so a free soul, freed from ego and attachment, works out his past Karma. He is free from entanglement with any future Karma.

" A man without self-control may run away from the world and the attractions of the world, but he can never run away from his own mind and passions. These follow him. But a man who is self-controlled and devoted to God may live in the world and yet not be of it.

" Thou who hast already taken shelter at the Lotus Feet of the Lord, and hast thus controlled thine enemies, the passions, shouldst remain in the world and do the will of the Lord."

When the divine Brahmā commands, the good obey ; Priyavrata bowed before him. His greatest desire was to serve God. Since it was the Lord's will that he should remain in the world and engage in the activities becoming to a ruler of the earth, he was content to have it so.

In time he took a wife, and to him were given ten sons and one daughter. Three of his sons were born free of any physical consciousness, and were therefore saints from birth. To them was granted a blessed exemption—they were not to experience the gross world of the senses, but were to dwell forever in the consciousness of God, knowing only the divine Self, the one Self, the Self of the universe.

Priyavrata, meanwhile, laboured zealously in behalf of his kingdom. It was he who among other achievements divided the earth into seven islands, and established thereon the seven kingdoms, over which he set his sons to rule. Indeed, he became so engrossed in temporal affairs that for a time he forgot his true and divine nature. A veil of ignorance floated like a cloud over his vision.

But happily this condition was not to continue. One day the veil lifted, the memory of his former delight in the life of the spirit revived, and there arose in him great spiritual insight and power of discrimination. He renounced all attachment, and soon realized the highest truth as taught by his beloved spiritual guide Nārada. And then, for a second and last time, his consciousness was united with God.

CHAPTER II

THE ROYAL SAGE RISHABHA

PRIYAVRATA'S grandson Nābhi, who had no children, wished above all things for a son. Hoping to gain the favour of God, he called together well-known priests of the temple to assist him in performing a sacrificial rite. Although God is not easily attainable either by sacrificial rites or ceremonial worship or forms or rituals, He freely bestows His gifts upon His true worshippers. Nābhi was one of these, and he was so loved of the Lord that scarcely had the ceremonial worship begun when the benign presence of God Himself was felt.

At once aware of that great presence, Nābhi and the officiating priests were overwhelmed with joy, and bowing themselves at the Lotus Feet of the Lord, they offered Him their hearts' worship. Then they sang His glory:

"O Thou worshipful Lord,
Thou art infinite, Thou lackest naught;
Yet Thou dost accept the worship of Thy children,
To shower Thy mercy upon them.
What praise can we sing of Thee?

We can only bow down at Thy Lotus
Feet,
Following the way of the wise.

"Thou art the Lord of the universe,
Beyond all name and form :
Who can express Thee, Thou who art inexpressible ?
Yet they sing the glory of Thy power,
For Thou dost charm away all evil.

"Beyond speech and mind art Thou, yet easily attainable by Thy devotees ;
Thou dost manifest Thyself to those who worship Thee in any name or form,
If only that worship is offered Thee with a sincere and devoted heart.

"Thou needest not worship for Thyself ;
Thou dost accept it to please Thy devotees and to crown their heart's desire.
The wise who take delight in Thee,
And have become one with Thee,
Whose hearts are purified by nonattachment,
And touched by the fire of knowledge,
Always sing Thy name and Thy glory.

"If because of evil Karma we walk the path of the unrighteous,

Deluded in the mire of ignorance,
Grant us this prayer, O Lord :
That we may sing Thy name,
Which charms away all sin and evil.
The veil of ignorance, difficult indeed to lift, keeps us from seeing Thy divine face.
Thy grace and the service of great souls make possible the easy crossing of Māyā."

Thus praising the Lord of all sacrifice, the priests performed their special oblations.

In due course, as a boon from God, a son was born to Nābhi, with all the auspicious marks of a potentially great soul. As the years passed by, the little child grew to be a young man, lovable, gifted, and self-controlled. He showed himself worthy of his great name, Rishabha,[1] for, possessing unusual strength both of mind and body, he excelled in every way. Moreover, the predictions attending his birth were now being justified, for gradually he was unfolding within himself the knowledge that there is one God in all beings and things.

---

[1] Rishabha means, literally, " one who excels all others."—Rishabha came to be regarded as the founder of Jainism. Mahāvīra, a contemporary of Buddha, is worshipped by the Jainas as the latest of the Jinas (spiritual heroes), and Rishabha as the first of them—of the present cycle.

As he came thus to look with an equal eye upon all, it was natural that he should, in turn, be loved equally by all his father's subjects, whether of high or low estate.

At last when, esteemed by all, he attained manhood, his father Nābhi abdicated in his favour. Released from the duties of kingship, Nābhi, with his wife, now retired to Badarikāśrama, the sacred retreat in the Himālayas. There they passed their days in meditation on the Lord in his aspect as Nara-Nārāyana, and ultimately realized their unity with him.

King Rishabha married Jayanti, a daughter of Indra, the King of the gods. They had many sons born to them, of whom Bharata was the eldest and wisest. This land is called Bhāratavarsha after him.

Rishabha was a free soul. He was pure in heart and had realized his oneness with the absolute, blissful consciousness. Yet he engaged in worldly activities for the good of humanity. He was the friend of all beings, kind, full of sympathy for all, self-controlled ; and, for the good of all, he taught rules of conduct for householders, following which all might attain freedom. His was an exemplary life. During his rule none of his subjects was in want : everyone had enough, and was content.

Once, during his wanderings, when the kingly sage Rishabha came to Brahmāvarta and there met his sons, who were studying with men of wisdom, he taught his sons these truths :

" Human birth is a blessed birth. Man must not run after the pleasures of the senses and be deluded. Such pleasures should have been enjoyed in the lower animal births ; a man ought not to waste this higher birth on such follies.

" For man, the practice of Tapas is the highest activity. Tapas purifies the heart. Blessed are the pure in heart, for they shall know the perfect joy.

" Association with holy men and service of great souls open the door to the kingdom of God. Association with the impure leads man to destruction.

" Great indeed are the souls who look with an equal eye upon all, who are tranquil and free from passions. They are the friends of all ; their conduct is always good. They have love for God, and they are not attached to the world. They ask for nothing more than the simple needs of the body.

" When man is attracted by the things of this world, and seeking pleasure, pursues them, he suffers delusion and engages in every kind of evil. Man is divine ; he is the divine Self. It is evil deeds that cause his identification with the physical body. Therefore he should desist from all evil.

"Man experiences suffering, misery, and death — all caused by ignorance — until he wakes up and seeks the divine Truth.

"Deeds attach themselves to the mind, and the mind causes physical bondage. Man, thus deceived by ignorance, is forced by the impulse of past impressions in the mind to repeat evil deeds. When he learns to take delight in the worship of the Lord of Love, he becomes free.

"Deluded in self-gratification, man does not realize the evil of running after the pleasures of sense. He remains forgetful of his true, divine, blissful nature, and by his attachment to worldly delights, causes his own sufferings.

"Sexual desire is the strongest of all desires, and its gratification causes delusion and creates a new tie. This tie is a bondage of the ego and with the idea of the ego there comes gross physical consciousness. When, through good deeds, the tie of sex is loosened, man begins to think of higher things ; he meditates on the divine Self, and thus freeing himself from ego, the cause of all bondages, he attains the supreme good.

"Follow me, thy supreme Teacher, the divine Self, the Brahman, with whole-souled devotion.[1]

"Be free from all selfish desires.

"Remain poised in the midst of the opposites of life.

"Love all beings as thyself.

"Seek and practise the truth.

"Desist from evil actions, and perform only those deeds which please and serve the Lord of Love.

"Associate with the holy, and converse about the Lord.

"Seek not praise for thyself.

"Give up all enmity and be friendly to all creatures.

"Practise self-control, and give up the ideas of 'me' and 'mine' with regard to this body and the objects of the world.

"Retire into solitude, and practise spiritual truths.

"Gain control over the Prāṇa, the senses, and the mind, and practise continence.

"Revere the great sages, and have faith in their words.

"Perform thy duties well.

---

[1] Rishabha, like Kapila in two earlier passages, in this line identifies himself with God. (See note, p. 44).

" Control thy speech.

" See Me everywhere and meditate on Me always, and thus shalt thou gain Self-knowledge.

" Be absorbed in the consciousness of God.

" Practise these truths with patience and perseverance. Above all be discriminative. Thus shalt thou be freed from ego and attain the kingdom of God.

" Alas, man does not know what is good for him. He seeks only the pleasures of sense, and, being deluded, does not realize that in seeking these passing pleasures he comes to great grief. The wise, who have realized the good, teach humanity because of the love and kindness in their hearts. He is the true teacher, and the true friend, who helps man out of darkness into light.

" God is infinite, the highest of the high, the dispenser of eternal happiness and freedom. By worshipping him alone, man becomes free from misery and from the great terror of death."

Having thus taught his sons, King Rishabha placed the eldest of them, Bharata, on the throne, and assumed the life of Sannyāsa. He wandered about in many places ; some honoured him and others abused him, but he remained undisturbed, for he had become established in the knowledge of the true, blissful, devine nature of the Self.

After he had meditated upon the Lord of Love and had realized his unity with Him who is the blissful Self of the universe, all the wonderful Yoga powers came to him. But he heeded them not. The wise know that the mind is not to be trusted. In unguarded moments it may betray even the greatest of Yogis or sages, if temptations are held before it. Yoga powers are great temptations.

Rishabha realized his oneness with God and freed himself from identification with his body. While yet living, he became a free soul. Just as a potter's wheel may go round a few times by its own momentum, so his body continued to live by the momentum of his past Karma. When that was exhausted Rishabha attained absolute freedom.

CHAPTER III

JADABHARATA

Bharata, son of the royal sage Rishabha, was a mighty monarch. He was so mighty that this land, which had been hitherto known as Ajanābha, was henceforth called Bhārata-varsha after his name.

Bharata ruled over his subjects like a kindly father who had the good of all his children at heart. He laboured incessantly for the benefit of all, but with no thought of personal gain; however slight the task, he performed it as a service to the Lord. Every act thus became one of devotion, purifying his heart, freeing him from passions, and finally uniting his consciousness with that of the supreme Brahman.

In his old age King Bharata divided his kingdom among his five sons and retired into the forest to meditate upon God, hoping thus to break the bonds of Karma which held him to life. He knew that all duties and all work are but preparation for the time when all the fetters which bind the soul to matter are forever cut asunder.

On the banks of the river Gaṇḍakī, in the forest of the Himālayas, he built himself a little cottage of reeds, and there, constantly meditating upon the God of Love, who resides in the souls of all men, he found that inner peace for which all his life he had striven.

Every morning he offered worship with the following prayer:

"May we meditate on the Supreme Light. From it the whole universe has issued. It exists in the hearts of all, and unto it will all go back. It is the intelligence in all beings.

It is the guide of all intelligence. In it do we take refuge."

Thus days, months, and years passed.[1] Then one day a doe came to drink water near the place where the royal sage was meditating. At the same moment, a little distance away, a lion roared. The doe was so terrified that she did not pause to satisfy her thirst but made a sudden jump to cross the river. Since she was with young, this extreme exertion and sudden fright made her give birth to a little fawn, and immediately afterward she dropped dead. The fawn fell into the water and was being swept away by the foaming stream when it caught the eyes of Bharata. Instantly the king rose from his meditation and rescued the newborn animal from the water. He took it to the cottage, made a fire, and with care and attention nursed the little thing back to life. Then the kindly sage took the fawn under his protection, bringing it up on soft grass and fruits. It thrived under the paternal care of the retired monarch and grew into a beautiful deer. Then he whose mind had been strong enough to break away from lifelong attachment to power, position, and family, became attached to the

---

[1] From this point to the end of the chapter the translation is that of Swami Vivekānanda, slightly revised.

deer which he had saved from the stream. And as he became more and more fond of the deer, the less and less could he concentrate upon the Lord. When the deer went out to graze in the forest and was late in returning, the royal sage would become anxious and worried. He would think, " Perhaps my little one has been attacked by some tiger or perhaps some other danger had befallen it ; otherwise, why is it late ? "

Some years passed in this way. Then one day, knowing that death was near, the royal sage laid himself down to die. But his mind, instead of being intent upon the Self, was thinking about the deer ; and while his eyes were fixed on the sad face of his beloved deer, his soul left the body. As a result of this, in the next birth he was born as a deer. But no Karma is lost, and all the great and good deeds done by him as a king and a sage bore their fruit. This deer was born jātismara. He remembered his past birth, though he was bereft of speech and was living in an animal body. He continually went apart from his companions, and was instinctively drawn to graze near hermitages where oblations were offered and the Upanishads were preached.

After the usual years of a deer's life had been spent, he died, and was born next as the youngest son of a rich Brahmin. In this life also he remembered all his past, and even in his infancy was determined to get entangled no more in the good and evil of life. As he grew up, he was strong and healthy, but he would not speak a word. He lived like one sluggish and weak-witted, from fear of getting entangled with worldly affairs. His thoughts were always on the Infinite, and he lived only to wear out his past Prārabdha-karma. In the course of time his father died, and the other sons divided the property among themselves. Thinking that the youngest son was a dumb, good-for-nothing young man, they seized his share. Their charity extended only to the point of giving him food enough to live on. The wives of the brothers were often very harsh with him, compelling him to do all the hard work, and if at any time he was unable to do everything they demanded, they would treat him very unkindly. But he showed neither vexation nor fear ; neither did he speak a word. When they persecuted him too much, he would stroll out of the house and sit under a tree, hour after hour, until their wrath was appeased, and then he would quietly go home again.

One day when the wives of his brothers had treated him with more than usual unkindness,

Bharata went out of the house, seated himself under the shadow of a tree, and rested. Now it happened that King Rahūgaṇa was passing by, carried in a palanquin on the shoulders of bearers. One of the bearers had unexpectedly fallen ill, and so the king's attendants were looking about for a man to replace him. They came upon Bharata seated under a tree, and, seeing he was strong, they asked him if he would take the place of the sick man.

Bharata did not reply, whereupon the king's servants caught hold of him and placed the pole on his shoulders. Without speaking a word, Bharata walked on with his fellow-bearers. Very soon after this the king remarked that the palanquin was not being carried evenly, and looking out of it he addressed the new bearer, saying: "Fool, rest awhile; if thy shoulders pain thee, rest awhile." Then Bharata, laying the pole of the palanquin down, opened his lips for the first time in his life, and spoke:

"Whom dost thou, O king, call a fool? Whom dost thou ask to lay down the palanquin? Whom dost thou say is weary? Whom dost thou address as 'thou'? If thou meanest, O king, by the word 'thou' this mass of flesh, it is composed of the same matter as thine; it is unconscious, and it knoweth no weariness, it knoweth no pain. If it is the mind, the mind is the same as thine ; it is universal. But if the word ' thou ' is applied to something beyond that, then it is the Self, the Reality in me, which is the same as in thee, and it is the One in the universe. Dost thou mean, O king, that the Self can ever be weary—that it can ever be tired—that it can ever be hurt ? I did not want, O king—this body did not want—to trample upon poor worms crawling on the road, and therefore as I tried to avoid them the palanquin moved unevenly. But the Self was never tired, it was never weak, it never bore the pole of the palanquin ; for it is omnipotent and omnipresent."

The king Rahūgaṇa, who was proud of his learning, knowledge, and philosophy, alighted from the palanquin and fell at the feet of Bharata, saying, " I ask thy pardon, O mighty one ; I did not know that thou was a sage when I asked thee to carry me. It is my great blessing that I met thee. Pray teach me the knowledge of Self."

" O king," said Bharata, " to know thy Self is the highest knowledge. But this knowledge of the Self does not arise so long as man thinks he can find happiness in the transitory world.

" Man remains bound by his own deeds, good or evil, because of the identification of the Self with the three Guṇas—Sattva, Rajas and Tamas. Good or evil attaches itself to the mind alone, and never to the true Self. The mind is like an adjunct to the Self. The divine Self appears as an individual spirit because of its association and identification with the mind. As are the deeds—good or evil—which attach themselves to the mind, so is the new birth, high or low. Man enjoys or suffers according to his deeds. The mind therefore, is the cause of bondage as well as the cause of freedom.

" Mind associated with the Guṇas becomes the cause of bondage and suffering ; but when freed from this association it brings freedom and peace.

" The eternal subject, the eternal witness, is the divine Self—untouched by any deeds or thoughts. It is beyond the mind and the senses. It is light itself. It is God—called Nārāyaṇa, for, ' He resides in the hearts of all beings.' He is Vāsudeva, for ' He is the refuge of all beings.' He is the ruler of His own Māyā and as ruler He dwells at the heart of all He has created.

" Human beings go round and round in the wheel of birth and death until they wake up, and, by controlling their passions, free themselves from the bondage of Māyā and know the truth about the Divine Self. There is no salvation or freedom until a man frees himself from his own mind, knowing the truth of the Self as distinct from the mind. It is the mind that causes all experience of misery, delusion, disease, lust, greed, and anger. The mind is the abode of all these. Subjugate this mind with the sword of knowledge made keen by the worship of the Lord of Love, the teacher of all teachers.

" There is one Truth, one existence—knowledge itself, the unitary consciousness, pure, unchangeable, beyond subject and object. This knowledge they call God—the Lord of Love.

" Not by mere study of the Vedas, nor by penance, nor even by good deeds, can one attain this knowledge, but by association with great souls. When the heart has become pure, one takes delight in meditating upon the Lord of Love. Burning the sin of ignorance in the fire of knowledge, man realizes his identity with Brahman, and attains the Lord of Love, the goal of life.

" Indeed, this world can be compared to a dense forest where men have lost their way. There are thieves and robbers in the forest—the senses and sense-experiences—which rob us of our true heritage, the divinity within. There is a mirage before us ; we see it and run to satisfy our thirst. There is the thirst for happiness in us, and we run to satisfy this in the objective world, which is as illusive as the mirage. At times we remember that there is nothing desirable in the world, but this we soon forget. We go round and round in this forest and do not find our way out until some kind traveller, some great soul, reveals it to us. The wise, the self-controlled ones, having attained freedom for themselves, show us the way to freedom.

" O king Rahūgaṇa, thou also art lost in the deep forest of the world. Give up all attachment, be friendly to all beings, and with the sword of Knowledge, sharpened by worship and meditation and service, cut asunder the bonds of ignorance."

Bharata having thus spoken, the king prostrated himself before him. Thereupon they took leave of each other. Bharata continued to teach the Truth that he had realized, and the king returned to his kingdom, there to realize the Truth which he had learned.

CHAPTER IV

TRUTH IS ONE : SAGES CALL IT BY VARIOUS NAMES

TRUTH is one : sages call it by various names. There is one God, one absolute Truth and one

Existence. People of different countries worship one God under various names and in different forms. Each of these names and forms is a face of the Infinite, and is one with the Infinite.

In Bhadrāśva-varsha,[1] Bhadrāśravas, the king, and his followers and attendants, worship the God of Love in His aspect as Hayagrīva, and praise His glory thus :

" Our salutations to Dharma, the embodiment of Truth ! Our salutations to Him who is the redeemer and purifier of our souls !

" Life is like a wind, that bloweth and is gone. Fleeting indeed is life ! Yet such is the inscrutable power of ignorance that man clings evermore to his existence, and wastes his energies on ephemeral pleasures. The wise alone realize within their heart of hearts the transitory nature of all things mortal, and they alone, in deepest contemplation, experience the Truth.

" Our salutations to Thee, O Lord !
Thy power is inscrutable ;
Thou art the Self of all,
Yet art Thou above and beyond all.

---

[1] The Eastern portion of the world as known to the ancients. All names ending with varsha, are names of countries.

When, at the time of the world's dissolution,
The Daitya, the embodiment of ignorance,
Stole away the Vedas, the divine knowledge,
Thou didst restore the Vedas from the depths of the nether regions.
Assuming the blissful form of Hayagrīva,
Thou didst establish the Truth once more,
Giving the Vedas and their knowledge to Thy son Brahmā.
Thou art Truth, and Thy desire is true :
Our salutations to Thee ! "

In Hari-varsha, the great devotee Prahlāda and his followers worship God in His aspect as Nṛ-Simha. They worship him with whole-souled devotion and unite their hearts with him in love. They sing his glory thus :

" Our salutations to Thee ! Thou art the infinite Lord,
Assuming the form of Nṛ-Simha ;
Thou art the Light of all lights.
Remove the darkness of ignorance from us ;
Burn all the seeds of our evil desires and evil Karmas ;
Make us fearless. We salute Thee !

" O Lord, shower Thy blessings upon all ;
May good come to all.

May those who have evil ways come to realize the good.
That they may follow the way of the good.
May all beings be kind and loving to one another ;
May all think good of one another ;
May all realize the good within themselves.
" May we not be attached to the things of the world ;
If attachment grow in our hearts,
Let it not be for relatives or friends
Other than those who are Thy lovers and devotees.
Thy lovers and devotees, the knowers of Truth,
Live in Thy blissful consciousness and sing Thy glories.
Association with such purifies the heart ;
Those who are pure in heart love Thee dearly,
And through their love obtain Thy grace and power.
" As water is the very life of fish,
So art Thou the life and soul of all beings.
Without Thee life is empty :
Vain indeed is life in this world,
The abode of misery and death,
Where prevail anger, sorrow, jealousy, pride, fear, and all evil.

But if one knows Thee his life becomes divine,
And his heart overflows with the fullness of its joy."

In Ketumāla-varsha, Lakshmī Devī, with her attendants, worships the infinite Lord as the Beloved and prays to him thus;

"Our salutations to Hrishīkeśa, the Lord of the senses,
Who is manifest in all that is good.
Thou art the Lord of all work,
The Lord of all knowledge,
The Lord of the mind and the Lord of all objects.
Thou art the embodiment of the Vedas,
Thou art life, Thou art immortality,
Thou art all in all.
Thou art courage,
Thou art the vigour of the senses,
Thou art the strength of the body,
Thou art desire,
We salute thee;
Thou art our beloved Lord."

In Ramyaka-varsha, the Lord of Love is worshipped in his divine manifestation as Matsya. Thus is he there addressed:

8

"Our salutations to thee, in thy divine aspect of Matsya,
The manifester of all strength, physical and mental.
Thou art within all beings, thou art also outside of all.
None knows thy nature.
Thou art the ruler of this universe.
Thou art the support and refuge of all."

In Hiraṇmaya-varsha, God is worshipped as Kūrma, and thus he is glorified :

"Our salutations to Kūrma !
Thou art omnipresent and the support of all.
Thou art beyond all space and time,
Thou art expressed in every being and in everything in this manifold universe,
Thy forms are innumerable,
Thy names are many,
Thou art that knowledge which gives awareness of unity.
We salute thee !"

In Uttarakuru-varsha, he is worshipped in his divine aspect as Varāha. Thus do they praise him :

"Our salutations to thee !
Thou art the Word, thou art the Truth,

Thou art the sacrifice, and thou art the
Sacrificial work ;
Thou art the Soul of all souls ;
As fire doth exist hidden in the wood,
So dost thou exist hidden in the body and
the senses,
With their hearts and minds purified by
spiritual discrimination and by virtuous
deeds,
The wise seek thee and find thee,
By thy Power, the divine Māyā,
It is thy Self that has become manifest as
this manifold universe.
In deep contemplation the self-controlled
realize thy absolute aspect.
We salute thee ! "

In Kimpurusha-varsha, the infinite Lord is worshipped in his divine incarnation as Rāma. The great devotee Hanumān and his followers worship the Lord with whole-souled devotion, and praise the glory of Rāma thus :

" Our salutations to Rāma !
In thee is manifest all that is highest ;
Thou art the embodiment and ideal of
purity and saintliness.
We take refuge at thy Feet, O Rāma,

Who art the incarnation of the universal
 Spirit.
That which the Scriptures indicate as the
 one blissful existence—
That thou art.
The pure unitary consciousness is thy
 nature;
Thou art beyond the known,
Beyond all name, all form, all attributes;
The pure in heart realize thee as one with
 Brahman.
Thou art the Self of the universe,
The Lord of all.
Thy delight is in thine own bliss;
Yet thou art born as the son of Daśaratha
To embody the living Truth on earth,
And to set before humanity the ideal of
 non-attachment.
Thou art the friend of the wise,
And the friend of those who love thee.
Vain indeed are good birth, position beauty,
 intelligence,
If there is no love for thee.
Grant this prayer, O Rāma—
That all may have love for thee
And realize thy everlasting peace and
 blessedness.
Thou art verily God, revealed as Rāma."

In Bhāratavarsha, God in his aspect as Nārāyaṇa has set forth the ideals of duty, service, renunciation, knowledge, self-control, non-egoism, and the realization of self-knowledge. The divine sage Nārada has taught this prayer to the Hindus of all colours and castes :

" Our salutation to Nara-Nārāyaṇa !
Thou art the Lord of the senses ;
Thou art the wealth of the poor,
The teacher of the wise,
The Lord of the saints who delight in meditation on the divine Self.

" Thou art the creator, preserver, and destroyer of this universe,
Yet thou art not the doer of any deed.
Thou dost exist in all bodies,
Yet the attributes of the body do not affect thee.
Thou art the seer and the knower of all objects,
Yet changing phenomena do not affect thy unchanging nature.
Thou art unattached and the knower of all,
Yet beyond all.

" O thou Lord of Yogis,
The secret and skill of all Yoga is to unite the mind with thee.

Through the Yoga of love to free ourselves
from ego :
That also is the secret of immortality.
Of what use is learning or the study of the
Scriptures
If one is still in fear of death,
In fear of separation from friends, relatives,
and possessions ?
The sway of Māyā is strong indeed :
Difficult it is to give up physical attachment.
Oh, teach us that secret of Yoga
Which will free us from all desire, from all
Māyā."

Human birth is of all births the highest. As human beings, we earn knowledge and freedom through whole-souled devotion to God. In India, the most sacred of all lands, are born great free souls. By mingling with such souls we learn to love God, the Soul of all souls. As our love for God increases, our ignorance vanishes. Then we ourselves become worthy of freedom.

We hold it a great privilege to be born in the sacred land of India. For here are nurtured the ideals of love, service, worship, meditation —all of which ideals lead to the realization in ourselves of God. Not for selfish purposes do the true worshippers of God dedicate themselves to him. The highest ideal—the one living ideal in India—is to love and worship him for the sake of love and wisdom only.

Love him, serve him, worship him, meditate on him with this ideal as your sole aim; thus shall you realize the highest good.

BOOK SIXTH

THE ARGUMENT

THE Sūta continues to relate, after Śuka, the *Bhāgavatam*. Here Vyāsa recounts ancient stories in illustration of spiritual truths.

CHAPTER I

THE STORY OF AJĀMILA

IF a man commits sinful acts which he does not expiate in this life, he must pay the penalty in the next life; and great will be his suffering. Therefore, with a self-controlled mind, a man should expiate his sins here on earth.

Expiation and repentence, to a man who continues to commit sinful acts knowing them to be harmful, are of no avail. Futile is to bathe an elephant if he is straightaway to roll again in the mud. All sinful thoughts and evil deeds are caused by ignorance. The expiation comes from illumination. As fire consumes all things, so does the fire of knowledge consume all evil and ignorance. Complete transformation of the inner life is necessary; and this is accomplished by control of the mind and the senses, by the practice of concentration, and by following and living the Truth.

The great secret of this complete transformation is the development of love for God. As when the sun rises the dewdrops vanish away, so when love grows all sin and ignorance disappear.

Even the most sinful man is purified if he surrenders himself to the God of Love and with whole-souled devotion serves his devotees. The path of love leads to the highest good, and is the easiest and simplest path by which to free ourselves from sin. Death is conquered, and the fear of death is overcome, by meditating upon the Lotus Feet of Krishna, the God of Love.

An ancient story tells how Ajāmila overcame death. Ajāmila, a Brahmin by birth, married a woman of low caste who had evil ways. An easy prey to wicked and sinful habits, he became very dishonest. Of his ten sons, the youngest, called Nārāyaṇa, after the name of God, was most dear to him.

Now when Ajāmila was lying near death he saw before him three ugly demon-figures ready to snatch his soul away from his body. These were the attendants of the King of Death. Ajāmila, terror-stricken called to his son Nārāyaṇa, but as he uttered the name of Nārāyaṇa his mind became concentrated on the Feet of Nārāyaṇa, the Lord of Love.

While he was thus meditating upon God, there appeared before him the attendants of Lord Viṣṇu. These opposed the attendants of Death.

Whereupon the latter asked :

" Why do you hinder us and thus prevent the Law from taking its course ? As a man sows, so must he reap. Man is subject to the three Guṇas, and since in one man one of them predominates, and in another man another, there are three classes of people in the world —the calm and peaceful, the active and restless, and the dull and indolent. Men are therefore either happy or miserable or both. The nature of their next lives is determined in the same way. The present life shows plainly their past, as well as their future. The ignorant sees only the present ; his vision being limited strictly to phenomena, he knows neither the past nor the future.

" Man is more than the physical body, more than he appears to be. His deeds all leave impressions in another part of him—his subtle body. These impressions control his actions, and his future life in turn is controlled by the deeds of his present life.

" We are the attendants of Death. We can read the past, present, and future of all beings. We are here to obey the Law, to see that the Law deals with this man according to his life here.

" Now this Brahmin Ajāmila was in his early youth a good and devout man. He was well-versed in the Scriptures, self-controlled, truthful, pure, a friend to all beings and to all creatures. But one day, while in the woods gathering flowers and leaves for worship, he chanced upon a young man and woman engaged in amorous play. Lustful desires were aroused in him. He lost all control over himself and became greatly attracted to the woman, who was of low caste and possessed of evil habits. Because of her, Ajāmila forsook his lawful wife and gave up the pure life that he had been living. He wasted his entire fortune trying to please this woman, and, when all was gone, he took to earning his living by various dishonest means. Many years of his life passed in this evil way. Now he is ready to die in his sins. He will be compelled to expiate his evil deeds, and we are here to take him to the King of Death, who will punish him justly. The suffering which he undergoes will in turn purify him."

The attendants of Viṣṇu replied:

"But this Brahmin has expiated all his sins by uttering the name of God and surrendering himself to the beloved Lord. One, however sinful, who loves God and surrenders himself to Him, is His beloved and His own. The mere name of God has power to save even the most depraved. Wrong-doing is not eradicated merely by expiation if the mind continues to follow wicked desires. But when the name of God and God's love have purified the heart, then indeed are all sins completely destroyed.

"You have no power over this man because he has freed himself from his evil deeds by chanting the name of God and surrendering himself at his Lotus Feet."

The attendants of Death, finding themselves bereft of power, went away.

Then Ajāmila regained his consciousness. He could still see the attendants of Viṣṇu before him, but while he was trying to express his love and gratitude to them they vanished.

Gradually Ajāmila got back his health. Then he thought within himself: "Truly a great blessing has been vouchsafed me. I have lived a very wicked life, yet through the infinite mercy of the Lord I have been granted the vision of the attendants of Lord Viṣṇu, perhaps because of a few good deeds stored up from my past. I feel that I am purified. My whole life seems transformed."

Evil ways no longer attracted him. He gave up all attachment to his wife, his children, his home, and went to live by the Ganges to practise Yoga. He attained control over his senses, and united his heart and mind with the divine Self. He practised concentration and meditation for many years, and his mind, like a steady light protected from the wind, became firmly fixed in the thought of God, the highest Self.

But at last death again approached him, and once more he saw before him the attendants of the Lord Viṣṇu. He prostrated himself before them, meditated upon the Lord, and gave up his body. He entered the chariot which awaited him and ascended with the attendants of Viṣṇu to the celestial sphere, where there are no more sorrows, nor disease, nor death.

By chanting the sacred name of God and meditating upon the Lord of Love, Ajāmila had freed himself from the bondage of Karma. Verily nothing is more purifying than the holy name of God.

CHAPTER II

DAKSHA'S PRAYER TO THE IMPERSONAL

DAKSHA, son of the Munis, worshipped God and sang his glory thus:

"Our salutations to the most high!
Pure consciousness is thy nature:
Thou art the ruler of Māyā and Lord of all beings.
They know not thy divine nature
Who live within the bonds of the Guṇas.
Who can define thee, who art self-existent and self-luminous?

"Objects seen know not the sense of sight,
Nor does any man know the true seer!
Thou art the seer, omniscient,
Dwelling in the hearts of all.

"We salute thee: thou art Hamsa, the pure spirit;

Thy nature is revealed in deepest contemplation,
When the mind becomes absorbed in thee
And soars beyond all consciousness of name and form.

"As fire remains hidden in wood,
So dost thou remain hidden in the body!
With heart and intellect absorbed in thee,
The wise find thee in thy hiding place.
Shower thy mercy upon us!

"Thou art the seer of thyself,
Thou dost experience thine own bliss,
Thou dost control thy Māyā, which bringeth forth this manifold universe.

"Thy power is infinite,
Thy form is universal,
Thou art the Soul in all beings and things.

"Words cannot express thee,
Intellect cannot know thee,
Senses cannot find thee,
Mind cannot conceive thee:
Thou art beyond all.

"Thou art the cause, thou art the effect;
Thou art the work, thou art the doer;
Thou art the instrument, thou art the action;

Thou art the cause of all causes :
Thou art all in all,
There is nothing beyond or above thee.
From thee all religions spring forth,
Thou art the source of all Scriptures,
Thou art the fountain of all knowledge ;
Yet none of these can fully reveal thy
infinite nature.
For verily thou art supreme ;
Infinite, absolute, impersonal, beyond all
name and form art thou.

" Thou art the boundless ocean of bliss :
As the formless ocean is affected by
intense cold
And moulded into various shapes,
So dost thou through the intense love of
thy worshippers
Assume countless names and innumerable
forms
To gladden their hearts.
Vouchsafe unto me that love out of thine
infinite mercy !

" Goodness is my form,[1]
Japam is my body,
Prayers are my limbs,

---

[1] Here Daksha suddenly identifies himself with God. (Cf. pp. 44, 98).

Tapas is my heart,
Virtue is my mind,
Sainthood is my vital energy :
I am existence, knowledge, and bliss
absolute."

CHAPTER III

NĀRADA TEACHES THE IDEAL OF RENUNCIATION

DAKSHA'S sons, known as Haryaśvas, who were exactly the same in character and mind, went to a sacred place called Nārāyaṇasaras, where the river Sindhu joins the ocean. There, living in the society of holy men, they attained purity of heart.

One day the divine sage Nārada approached them and said :

" O Haryaśvas, do you know the end of the field? Without knowing the end of the field all austerities are fruitless.

" There is a kingdom where reigns the one and only king. There is a well whence there is no return.

" There is a woman who assumes many forms. There is one who is the husband of the woman.

"There is a river which flows in opposite directions. There is a house which is built of twenty-five kinds of material.

"There is a bird which has great discrimination and which twitters beautiful songs. There is an object which is in perpetual motion.

"When you understand what these are, you will know the Truth and become free."

Hearing these puzzling words from Nārada, the sons of Daksha meditated upon them, and from within themselves came the answer.

"The field is the ego. By reaching the end of one's ego, one realizes the divine Self and attains freedom.

"The kingdom is this universe, of which God is the supreme king and ruler. Until we know that ever-free One and surrender our hearts to him, all our struggles are in vain. God, the light of all lights, is the well, and after finding him we are born no more.

"The woman is the mind, which assumes many forms of waves, according to the working of the different Guṇas. The husband is the divine Self, which, by identifying itself with the mind, is caught in the meshes of the Guṇas. As a husband loses his independence through association with an overbearing wife, so the Self loses its freedom by becoming a slave to the mind, and then it experiences the opposites—happiness and misery, life and death.

" The river is the river of Māyā, and so long as we remain in the current of this Māyā we know no freedom.[1]

" The physical, subtle, and causal bodies form the house, whose twenty-five materials are twenty-five categories: and therein the Self resides.

" The Scriptures are the discriminative bird, for they teach us by means of divine songs to judge between the real and the unreal.

" Time is the object in perpetual motion which causes the whole universe to move.

" By rising above all idea of motion, or time, we find peace."

When the Haryaśvas realized the truth of the words spoken by Nārada, they followed the path of Brahman and attained their absolute freedom.

CHAPTER IV

THE STORY OF CHITRAKETU

HUMAN birth, O king, is indeed a blessed birth, because it is an evolution into self-consciousness which gives the incentive to all further

[1] The river of Māyā flows in opposite directions, leading people either towards greater bondage or towards liberation.

growth. Man alone is able to know the highest Truth and attain perfection ; but alas, how few men even try to know what is good for them ! Fewer have any desire for freedom ; and fewer still learn the Truth and become free. Rare indeed are the calm souls who have realized the highest good by uniting their hearts with God.

I will tell you an ancient story to illustrate the truth I wish to teach.

Once there lived in Śūrasena a well-known king named Chitraketu. Every longing of his heart was fulfilled—save one ; but, not having this, he was unhappy. Neither his vast wealth, nor his beautiful wife, nor his youthful vigour, nor his many mistresses, could satisfy him. He desired a son.

One day the great sage Angira visited the court, and observing that the king was sad at heart, addressed him thus, seeking the reason for his sorrow :

" He who has conquered his own mind has conquered the universe. You look sad : it appears that you have some unfulfilled desire."

With deep respect for the sage the king replied :

" Revered master, you are a great Yogi. You have burnt all your impurities in the fire of Yoga. You have become omniscient, and you know the innermost thoughts of all. You therefore know my thoughts and desires, but since you appear to wish me to express them, I will do so : I have everything that a man can desire except that which would complete my happiness. I have no son."

The sage Angira felt pity for the king and blessed him and his queen. As the sage was leaving, he said, " You shall have a son born to you, O king, but he will cause you much grief as well as happiness."

In due course a son was born to him, and King Chitraketu's joy knew no bounds. There was gladness in the hearts of all. But the gladness soon turned to sorrow when one day the nurse found the child lying dead. He had been poisoned by the jealous mistresses of the king.

The king's anguish was unbearable. And now once again the sage Angira, accompanied this time by the divine seer Nārada, came before him, and said :

" For whom art thou grieving, O king? He whom thou didst call thy son is not dead. Like sand in a river, souls, carried by the stream of time, meet one another, and are swept apart. There is birth and there is death only for the bodies of men. The soul is immortal."

King Chitraketu felt greatly calmed in the

presence of the two great sages, and said :

" Who are you, O holy men ? Sages like you wander about the earth shedding the light of knowledge and peace whenever there is unrest and ignorance. Deign to shed that light upon me that all my ignorance may disappear."

" I am he," said Angira, " who blessed you with the child. The divine sage Nārada has come to give you his blessing also. We learned of the death of your beloved son and knew that you had been thrown into darkness because of your sorrow. You are a great devotee of the God of Love. You must not grieve thus.

" I might have granted you the highest illumination when I came to see you before, but then your only desire was for a son, and so I blessed you with a child. Now you have learned what it means to desire a son. Everything in life is transitory. Wealth, health, family, children—all are but a vanishing dream. All sorrow and grief are caused by attachment to them and desire for them. Even sorrow, and grief, and delusion, and fear, are transitory.

" Give up belief in the myriad opposites of life. Learn to discriminate. Know the one Truth alone and find peace.

" I am giving you a sacred Mantram, the name of God. Repeat the Mantram and meditate on it. Meditate on God with a self-controlled and concentrated mind, and you will soon rise above all sorrow and find ineffable peace."

Then the spirit of the dead child appeared to the divine sage Nārada, who entreated him to re-enter his dead body, live the allotted span of life on earth, and gladden the hearts of his parents and friends.

But the spirit replied:

"Who is my mother? Who is my father? I have neither birth nor death. I am the eternal spirit. The soul, subject to Karma, travels through many births and many forms. Caged in bodies, he is compelled through ignorance to experience the various earthly relationships. But I have known myself as the unchangeable, birthless, and deathless spirit. I am he, the eternal spirit, who forever remains untouched, unaffected by the love or hatred, the good or evil, of this universe. I am the eternal Witness. I am HE!"

Then the spirit disappeared. A sense of freedom from attachment and grief came to the sorrowing parents, and they performed the last rites for the dead body of their child.

Consoled by the wisdom of Nārada and Angira, King Chitraketu prostrated himself at the feet of these divine sages. They had brought to him that knowledge which gives peace. Nārada then initiated him into the sacred mysteries of meditation and taught him the following prayer:

"We bow down to thee:
Supreme bliss is thy form;
Intelligence itself is thy nature;
Thou art peace, and thy delight is in thyself;
Thou art beyond all human consciousness.

"Thou dost experience thine own bliss;
Attachment, delusion, or the working of thine own Māyā doth not affect thee;
Thou art supreme, the Lord of the senses and of all objects;
Thy faces are infinite.
We salute thee.
Where the mind and the senses seek in vain to reach thee,
There art thou expressed in thy divine glory;
Thou art nameless and formless;
Life and consciousness art thou,
The cause of all causes.
Do thou protect us and guide us.

"Like the all-pervading ether,
Thou art everywhere and within all;
Yet we know thee not.

The senses, mind, and intellect are astir
with conscious life
Because of the borrowed light of thy consciousness—
Even as iron gives out heat when it is
near the fire.
One realizes thee by going beyond the
senses, the mind, and the intellect.
May our hearts be drawn to thee!"

King Chitraketu began to practise the spiritual lessons taught him by the divine sages Angira and Nārada. Soon his mind was illumined, and he had the vision of the God of Love. He felt overwhelming joy in his heart, and attained peace and tranquillity.

As he continued his practices there came greater and greater illumination, and he ultimately realized his unity with Brahman:[1]

"I am he, the Self of the universe, dwelling in the hearts of all. I am the World. I am supreme Brahman.

"I exist as the Self of the universe, and the whole universe exists in me.

"Mind assumes three states of consciousness—waking, dreaming, and dreamless sleep. I am the witness thereof, remaining aloof from

[1] The verses that follow, spoken by the king express his unity with God. (See note, p. 98).

all these states, for I am transcendental consciousness.

"The blissful Self am I, experienced by transcending the senses, the mind, the intellect, and the ego. I am Brahman.

"As one sees oneself separate from Brahman, one comes within the domain of Māyā. Thus does one become subject to birth and death, and passes from one body to another.

"It is man's greatest calamity not to comprehend the divine Self.

"Man struggles to find happiness and to end his misery in this world, but he never attains this goal so long as he remains within the limits of the states of consciousness—waking, dreaming, and dreamless sleep. By transcending these and going beyond the world of Māyā, he realizes the Self and attains his goal.

"He who is skilful in the practice of Yoga and meditation comes to know that the supreme end of life is to realize unity with God."

BOOK SEVENTH

THE ARGUMENT

THE Sūta continues to relate, after Śuka, the *Bhāgavatam*. Here are set forth the teachings of Nārada, including an illustrative story.

CHAPTER I

THE STORY OF PRAHLĀDA

NARADA, while teaching divine wisdom to Yudhishthira, said :

God is to be meditated upon. Through constant meditation one attains to Truth : man is united with God, and human life is transformed into divine life. Just as a cockroach, when caught by a black bee, constantly thinks of the bee through fear, and finally becomes a bee itself, so by constantly thinking of God one becomes divine.

I will tell you a story which illustrates this truth :[1]

Hiraṇyakaśipu was the king of the Daityas, who, though born of the same parentage as the Devas or gods, were always at war with them. The Daityas had no part in the oblations and offerings of mankind, or in the government and guidance of the world. But at one time they waxed strong and drove the Devas from the heavens, and seized the throne of the gods, and so ruled for a period. Then the Devas prayed to Viṣṇu, the omniscient Lord of the universe, who helped them to drive out the Daityas ; and once more the gods reigned. Later, however,

---

[1] The translation is that of Swāmi Vivekananda, slightly revised.

after a considerable lapse of time, Hiraṇyakaśipu, still king of the Daityas, again succeeded in conquering his cousins, the Devas ; and seating himself on the throne of the heavens, he ruled the three worlds—the middle world, inhabited by men and animals ; the heavens, inhabited by gods and god-like beings ; and the nether world, inhabited by the Daityas. Now Hiraṇyakaśipu, declaring himself to be the God of the whole universe, proclaimed that there was no other god but himself, and strictly enjoined that the omnipotent Viṣṇu should have no worship offered to him anywhere, but that all worship should henceforth be given to himself only.

Hiraṇyakaśipu had a son called Prahlāda. It so happened that this Prahlāda, from his infancy, was devoted to Viṣṇu. And now the king, seeing that the evil he wanted to drive away from the world gave signs of cropping up, in his own family, made over his son to two teachers, called Shanda and Amarka—very stern disciplinarians—with strict injunctions that Prahlāda was never to hear the name of Lord Vṣṇu mentioned. These teachers took the prince to their home, and there he was put to study with other children of his own age. But the little Prahlāda, instead of learning from his books, devoted all his time to telling his schoolmates how to worship Viṣṇu. When his masters found this out, they were frightened, for they had great fear of the mighty king Hiraṇyakaśipu, and they now did their best to dissuade the child from his ways. But Prahlāda could no more stop his teaching and his worshipping of Viṣṇu than he could stop breathing. To clear themselves, Shanda and Amarka thought best to tell the terrible fact to the king—that his son was not only worshipping Viṣṇu himself but was corrupting all the other children by teaching them to do the same.

The monarch was very much enraged when he heard this, called the boy to his presence, and tried by gentle persuasions to dissuade him from the worship of Viṣṇu, teaching him that he, the king, was the only God to worship. But it was to no purpose. The child declared again and again that the omnipresent Viṣṇu, Lord of the universe, was the only being to be worshipped; for even he, the king, held his throne only so long as it pleased Viṣṇu. "Vain indeed is all pride in the conquest even of the whole universe," said Prahlāda, "if one has not conquered one's own passions. An uncontrolled mind is indeed our greatest enemy. The greatest conquest is the conquest of our own minds."

The anger of the king knew no bounds, and he ordered the boy to be immediately put to death. Thereupon, the Daityas struck him with pointed weapons ; but Prahlāda's mind was so intent upon Viṣṇu that he felt no pain from them.

When his father saw that it was so, he became frightened, but roused to the worst passions of a Daitya, contrived various diabolical means to kill the boy. He ordered him to be trampled under foot by an elephant. The enraged elephant, however, could not crush the boy any more than he could have crushed a block of iron. So this measure also was to no purpose. Then the king ordered the boy to be thrown over a precipice, which order too was duly carried out ; but, with Viṣṇu residing in his heart, Prahlāda came down upon the earth as gently as a flower drops upon the grass. Poison, fire, starvation, throwing into a well, enchantments, and other measures were then tried on the child, one after another, but to no avail. Nothing could hurt him in whose heart dwelt Viṣṇu.

At last, the king ordered the boy to be tied with mighty serpents called up from the nether worlds, and then to be cast to the bottom of the ocean, where huge mountains were to be piled high upon him, so that in the course of time, if not immediately, he would die. Even though treated in this manner, the boy prayed to his beloved Viṣṇu : " Salutations to thee, Lord of the universe, thou beautiful Viṣṇu." Thus thinking and meditating on Viṣṇu, he felt that Viṣṇu was near him—nay, that Viṣṇu was in his very soul—until at last he began to be conscious that he was Viṣṇu, and that he was everything and everywhere.

As soon as he realized this, all the snake-bonds snapped asunder, the mountains were pulverized, the ocean was upheaved, and he was gently lifted up above the waves and carried safely to the shore. As Prahlāda stood there he forgot that he was a Daitya and had a mortal body ; he felt that he was universe and that all the powers of the universe emanated from him ; he, himself, was the ruler of nature. Time passed thus, in one unbroken ecstasy of bliss, until gradually Prahlāda began to remember that he had a body, and that he was Prahlāda. As soon as he became once more conscious of his body, he saw that God was within and without ; and everything appeared to him as Viṣṇu.

When the King Hiraṇyakaśipu found to his dismay that all forcible means of getting rid of this boy—so irretrievably devoted to his enemy, the God Viṣṇu—had failed, he was at a loss to know what to do. He had the boy again brought before him, and tried once more by gentle words to persuade him to listen to his advice. But Prahlāda made the same reply as before. Then, thinking that the strange obstinacy of the boy would vanish with age and further training, he put him for a second time in charge of the teachers Shanda and Amarka, asking them to instruct him in the duties of a king. But the lessons did not please Prahlāda, and again he spent his time telling his schoolmates about the path of devotion to the Lord Viṣṇu.

When his father came to hear about it, he was again filled with rage, and, calling the boy to him, abused Viṣṇu in the most disgraceful terms possible, threatening at the same time to kill Prahlāda. But Prahlāda still persisted in maintaining that Viṣṇu was the Lord of the universe, without beginning, without end, omnipotent and omnipresent, and that, as such, he alone was to be worshipped. Then the king roared with fury, saying, "Thou evil one, if thy Viṣṇu is God omnipresent, why doth he not reside in that pillar yonder?" Prahlāda humbly replied that Viṣṇu was indeed there. "If so," cried the king, "let him defend thee," and, turning to the pillar he shouted, "I will kill thee with this sword." With that he rushed at the pillar and dealt a terrific blow. Instantly a thundering voice was heard, and lo, Viṣṇu issued forth from the pillar in his awful Nrisimha form — half lion, half man. Panic-stricken, the Daityas, except the king, ran away in all directions ; Hiraṇyakaśipu, refusing to fly, remained to fight single-handed with Lord Viṣṇu. Long and desperately they fought until at last King Hiraṇyakaśipu was overpowered and slain.

Then the gods descended from heaven and offered hymns to Viṣṇu, and Prahlāda fell at his Feet and broke forth into rapturous hymns of praise and devotion. And he heard the voice of God saying : " Ask, Prahlāda, ask for anything thou desirest. Thou art my favourite child ; ask therefore for anything thou mayest wish." Prahlāda, overcome with emotion replied : " Lord, I have seen thee. What else can I want ? Do thou not tempt me with earthly or heavenly boons." Again the voice said : " Nay, ask something, my son." And then Prahlāda replied :

" That intense love, O Lord, which the ignorant bear to worldly things, may I have the same for thee ; may I have the same intensity of love for thee, but only for love's sake."

Then said the Lord : " Prahlāda, though my devotees never desire anything, here or hereafter, yet by my command do thou enjoy the blessings of this world to the end of the present cycle, and with thy heart fixed on me perform works of religious merit. And thus in time, after the dissolution of thy body, thou shalt attain me." Thus blessing Prahlāda, the Lord Viṣṇu disappeared. Then the gods, headed by Brahmā, installed Prahlāda on the throne of the Daityas and returned to their respective spheres.

CHAPTER II

THE STAGES OF LIFE

YUDHISHTHIRA then inquired about the duties in the several stages of life. In answer Nārada continued :

The chief purpose of all religious observances and spiritual practices is self-control and perfection in meditation.

This body has been compared to a chariot. The senses are the horses. Mind is the rein. Intellect is the charioteer. The vital energies are the wheels. Virtue and vice are the spokes. Objects of the senses form the road. The ego is the rider. Anger, hatred, jealousy, sorrow, greed, delusion, pride, and thirst for life are the enemies met along the road. When the rider can bring the horses and the chariot under control, his heart becomes pure, and he finds divine grace within. With the sword of discrimination, sharpened by knowledge, he conquers all enemies. He becomes fearless and enjoys divine bliss.

Certain virtues there are which must be cultivated by all humanity in all stages of life. These are truthfulness, kindness, forgiveness, discrimination, control of the mind, mastery over passions, non-injury, continence, charity, frankness, contentment, devotion to spiritual teachers, desisting from idle conversation, seeking the highest Truth, serving all beings as God.

Certain truths also there are, revealed through the experiences of the sages, which must be heeded by all humanity. Human birth is the door through which we may attain higher or lower births according to our deeds. Human birth is also the door through which we may attain the highest goal of life, absolute freedom.

When man gives up the struggle for happiness through the doors of the senses, and learns to look within, then only does he find peace and bliss.

Clinging to wealth and clinging to worldly life are the root causes of all fear, misery, and delusion. Man should therefore give up seeking for wealth and longing for the pleasures of the world.

The bee undergoes many hardships to gather honey : men steal that honey. Likewise, those who struggle to earn and hoard wealth seldom enjoy it themselves.

The king of the snakes does not struggle to seek food ; he is satisfied with whatever nature provides for him. So also lives the sage. Whatever comes of itself, he accepts. Sometimes he sleeps under a tree ; sometimes he dwells in a palace. Under all conditions he is the same happy person.

Learn to be contented under all circumstances. One who has contentment in his heart finds good everywhere and at all times.

Those who wear shoes to protect their feet are not hurt by the thorns that lie upon the road. Likewise, those who have learned to be contented under all conditions are never hurt by the thorns that lie upon the path of life.

Discontentment is the cause of restlessness and passionate desires. Where discontentment exists, all effort, all learning, all fame or glory or knowledge, are in vain. The discontented heart is full of thirst and greed even when all the enjoyments of the whole world are at hand. Many a soul has become degraded because of discontentment.

Give up craving for the things of this world, give up greed; and so free yourself from anger. Learn the evanescence of all pleasures of the senses. Seek the divine consciousness, the knowledge of unity, and thus conquer all fear.

Learn to discriminate between the real and the unreal, and thus be free from sorrow and delusion.

Conquer pride and egotism by serving the great sages, the spiritual leaders, the embodiments of purity and holiness.

Banish the obstacles on the path of meditation by the control of speech and thought.

If any person does harm to you, do not seek to return the injury, nor even feel any resentment in your heart, but rather think good of him, for love conquers hatred.

He who earnestly seeks to achieve self-control must withdraw from worldly distractions. He must be moderate in eating, drinking, and recreation. Indolence he must shun.

In the first stage of life, one desiring self-control must enter upon the life of a student. The Guru removes from him the darkness of ignorance and reveals to him the light of knowledge. To prepare for the instruction to be given by the teacher, the student must achieve calmness and steadiness of body and mind.

He must free himself from physical ailments by the practice of such breathing exercises as may be given by the teacher, and by taking only such food as will maintain vigour in the body and calmness in the mind.

Sitting erect, in a position of controlled ease, he must repeat the sacred word OM—meditating on its meaning.

He must free the mind from all distracting thoughts and desires. When the mind wanders, let him bring it back and try to fix it on the divine light within the etheric centre of the heart.

Constant practice will bring tranquillity and peace within. The flame of desire will be extinguished, just as a fire goes down when no fuel is added.

The mind which is no longer agitated by lust is always tranquil. As the restless waves of the mind subside, there arises gradually divine bliss.

The sacred word OM is the bow. The purified mind is the arrow. The divine Self is the target. Just as the arrow becomes one with the target, so by the practice of concentration does the mind become united with the divine Self.

If one has devotion for his Guru as for God, he will easily gain control and mastery. The

Guru is truly one with God. Living in close association with the teacher, following his instructions in meditation and in the understanding of the Scriptures, the student learns to see God, the Soul of all souls, in all beings.

After finishing his course of study, he is free to marry and become a householder, or he may lead a life of retirement, or he may become a wandering monk, according to his particular temperament and the direction of his teacher.

The family man, who has to meet obligations in social life, must perform all duties as a form of worship. He must revere spiritual teachers and seek association with the holy. He must pass leisure hours in hearing or studying the Word of God. He must engage in the activities of life, but he must keep his mind free from all attachments.

He may possess wealth but he must regard himself as a trustee of God, to whom everything belongs. He must look to the needs of the poor and the destitute and serve the Lord in serving all sentient beings.

He must not be attached to the flesh and the pleasures of the senses. He must learn discrimination and realize the joy of life in the Spirit and know the glory of the divine Self within.

The wandering monk may go where he will but must not become attached to any place or country. He must learn to find peace and joy in meditation on the Ātman, the divine Self. In his eyes all beings must be equal. He must know the Lord to be the supreme goal and end of life. He must meditate upon the Scriptures and avoid studies which divert the mind from God.

He must never make disciples by force, or by tempting with false promises.

For a monk to yield to lustful desires, and for a family man to renounce the duties of life —both things are shameful, heinous, and deceitful.

The highest duty of life is to take delight in the Word of God and to meditate constantly upon him as the embodiment of all Truth.

Chant the name and praise of the Lord, and sing his glory. Meditate on his divine attributes ; constantly remember him and his Presence. Serve and worship the Lord of Love. Bow down to him ; know him as the true friend ; surrender yourself unto him.

The whole universe may be compared to a large tree. All beings may be said to be its leaves and branches. Hari, God, is the root of the tree. When the Lord is worshipped, all beings rejoice.

The Lord is all-pervading. He exists both in the sentient and in the insentient. Every country is his country, and he is manifest everywhere, but the most sacred places are where worship is offered to him—in temples or in the hearts of his devotees.

Those who desire the highest good should live where they may mingle with holy people.

Hari is also called the Purusha, the dweller within, for he resides in the hearts of all beings—in gods and angels, in men, in birds and beasts, and in every apparently insentient object. But though he resides in all creatures and things, there is a difference in the degree of his manifestation in them.

In human beings he is more manifest than in others. Again, among human beings he is more or less manifest according to the degree of knowledge or consciousness that is realized.

A wise Brahmin said : " After many experiences of happiness and misery, I have come to the realization that the Ātman is bliss, and that man is the Ātman. When man ceases to struggle for happiness in worldly pursuits, and learns to look within, he finds the blissful Ātman.

" The Ātman alone IS, One without a second. The Ātman alone is Reality. He is deluded indeed who knows not the Real.

" To attain the Ātman, give up the consciousness of the many and become absorbed in the One.

" Learn to see the One in the many. The process of practising and realizing this unity consists in seeing cause and effect as one and the same, in seeing the whole universe as an expression of God. The process of realizing unity in action consists in surrendering all words, deeds, and thoughts to Brahman, or God.

" The process of realizing unity in objects and persons consists in seeing God in all beings and things.

" He who follows the path of the contemplative life knows his Self as divine and as one with God. God is the beginning, he is the middle, and he is the end. He is the enjoyer and he is the object enjoyed. He is the high and he is the low. He is the knower and he is the known. He is the word spoken and he is the breath which speaks it. He is the manifest and he is the unmanifest.

" The man following this path realizes that God alone IS, that there is nothing apart from him or beyond him. Having realized this truth, the devotee is no longer attracted by the things of the world.

" He who is calm and feels the same towards all beings is a free soul. Though his wisdom is profound, his simplicity is childlike."

BOOK EIGHTH

THE ARGUMENT

THE Sūta continues to relate, after Śuka, the *Bhāgavatam*. This part consists of " The Story of the Dwarf."

CHAPTER I

A PRAYER

EVEN as rivers spring from different sources,
Yet mingle in the ocean,
So all the Vedas, all Scriptures, all Truth,
  though of diverse origin,
Come home to thee !

CHAPTER II

THE STORY OF THE DWARF

BALI, the king of the Asuras, was invincible for he had the grace of God on his side. He dethroned Indra, king of the Devas, took possession of his kingdom, and became the monarch of the three worlds.

Aditi, the beloved mother of Indra, was lamenting her son's defeat, when Kaśyapa, her husband, returned home after a long absence.

Kaśyapa felt very sorry for his wife, and sought to comfort her by saying: "Inscrutable is the power of Māyā. All beings are deluded by false attachments, O my beloved, know thy Self and be free. There is but one all-pervading existence, the blissful Ātman.

"Worship Vāsudeva, the God of Love, the innermost Self in all beings. Through his grace shalt thou be free from delusion."

"Teach me," then said Aditi, "how I may worship the great teacher of all teachers, the Lord of the universe, that he may fulfil the desire of my heart. Teach me how I may please the Lord, so that he will grant me whatever boon I may ask."

"Gladly will I teach you, O Aditi, how to please the Lord by service and worship, even as I have learned from Brahma, the son of God.

"God is to be worshipped with whole-souled devotion and to be meditated upon with focussed mind. Feel his living presence and make obeisance unto him with the following sacred prayers:

"Thou art Lord Vāsudeva, the Supreme
Being,
The witness, the refuge of all.
Thou art shining in the hearts of all.
Obeisance unto Thee!

"Unmanifest art Thou, beyond all knowledge
For Thou art the source of all knowledge.
Obeisance unto Thee!

"Thou art the sacrifice, and Thou art the
giver of the fruits of the sacrifice;
The wisdom of the Vedas is Thy very soul.
Thee we salute!

"Thou art the compassionate father,
Thou art the loving mother,
Thou art power, and Thou art knowledge:
The Lord of all beings.
Thee we salute!

"Thou art life,
Thou art intelligence,
Thou art the centre and soul of every sphere.
Thou art attainable by those who practise
Thy Yoga in sincerity,
Obeisance unto Thee!

"Thou art the God of all gods,
The Eternal Witness;

Thou art the sage Nārāyaṇa,
Thou art Hara, and Thou art Hari.
We salute Thee!

"Thou art Keśava, the Lord of Love;
Thy form is universal;
Eternal prosperity is Thy consort.
Obeisance unto Thee!

"Thou art the supreme refuge,
The giver of the highest boon,
Thou worshipful Lord;
The wise worship Thy Lotus Feet,
Desiring to attain the highest.
May it please Thee to shower Thy mercy upon us!

"Thus praising the glory of the Lord, fix thy mind on him. Associate with the holy and please them by service. Serve all beings as embodiments of the divine."

Thus taught by the sage Kaśyapa, Aditi shunned all indolence and devoted herself earnestly to worship of the Lord and to meditate upon him. She brought all her passions under control; her mind was stilled, and in her heart she realized the presence of the all-pervading Vāsudeva, the Soul of all souls. Great was her happiness! She was completely absorbed in that one presence; her heart melted in love, and she prayed:

"Thou art Holiness;
Holiness is Thy name.
Thou art the friend of the poor and lowly.
Thou art manifest in the hearts of all
Who take shelter at Thy Lotus Feet;
They are purified by Thy holy presence.
"Thou art the highest of the high;
Thy peace reigneth in the universe.
Associating Thyself with Thy divine Maya,
Thou dost create, preserve, and dissolve this universe;
Yet thou existest in Thine own primal glory, pure and absolute.
Obeisance unto Thee!
"O Thou infinite blissful existence,
If Thou art pleased,
Thou dost bestow all Thy glory, Thy power, and Thy grace upon Thy devotees."

Aditi felt a stillness within, and in the silence of her heart she heard the voice of God saying unto her:

"O thou mother of the Devas, I know what thou seekest. Thou desirest the victory of thy sons over Bali, the king of the Asuras. But Bali is now under the protection of my power. I am, however, pleased with thee; and thy desire shall be fulfilled, but in what manner I will not reveal. But this I will tell thee : my power will be born in thy womb as thy son."

In due course, this promise was fulfilled, and a son, with all the auspicious marks of a divine man, was born to Kaśyapa and Aditi. The son, however, was a dwarf. He became known as the dwarf Brahmin.

Bali, still king of the three worlds, held a great sacrifice, to which all the Brahmins were invited.

The dwarf set out to attend the ceremony. As he approached the place where the sacrifice was being prepared, all the wise Brahmins and Bali marvelled at the radiance which they saw illuminating the whole region. Soon they found out that the radiance proceeded from the dwarf. Then they all stood up in reverence, and Bali prostrated himself at his feet. Bali then addressed the dwarf, saying :

"Obeisance unto thee, Brahmin. Thou art the embodiment of all the divine powers. By thy holy presence I am blessed, and blessed indeed are my forefathers also. Blessed are all the three worlds by thy grace. Tell me thy wish, that I may please and serve thee."

To this the dwarf replied : "I am much pleased by thy reverence. It is befitting thee, for thou art the grandson of Prahlāda, the greatest of the devotees who have blessed this world. Thou hast promised me any gift which I may choose. Grant me only three steps of ground."

Bali laughed at this trivial request. " Oh, why ask for three steps of ground ? " He said. " I can give thee a large island or a big estate, so that thou mayest live in comfort with all thy needs supplied ; I pray thee, ask for a greater boon."

The dwarf smiled, in turn, and replied : " I shall be satisfied with as much space as can be covered with three steps ; I do not seek for more."

Bali continued to be amused by this foolish desire of the dwarf and said : " Thy desire is granted. May it please thee to accept the boon."

At this moment Sukrāchārya, the priest of Bali, intervened, saying, " What calamity hast thou brought unto thyself by thy promise of this gift ? Dost thou not see that this dwarf, born of Kaśyapa and Aditi, is the embodiment of the divine power ? He can cover the whole universe with his form, and thou wilt lose everything. Thou hast given everything to him ; there is nothing left for thee. He will give back the kingdom of the three worlds to Indra, the eldest of the Devas. One step of this dwarf will cover the earth, a second step will cover the heaven, and his form will cover the rest of the universe; there will be nothing left for his third step. It is not even in thy power to keep thy word!"

Bali now realized the gravity of his promise, but there was no help. He said, "I am not sorry for my promise of a gift to this dwarf. I must keep it. Am I not born in the family of Prahlāda?"

Now Bali turned to the dwarf, and with great reverence said; "Please accept the gift." Then as he again looked at the dwarf, he found the whole universe existing in him. As the dwarf then advanced his first step, behold, he covered the whole earth; his body covered the sky, and his arms embraced the four directions. With his second step, he covered the heavens and the rest of the universe. There was no room anywhere for his next step. Whereupon the dwarf smilingly looked at Bali and asked, "Now where may I take my third step?"

Bali humbly and reverently said: "I must keep my word. True, there is no more space in the whole universe for your next step—but here is my head. Place thy foot on my head, for I am thine for ever.

"Thy Feet, O Lord, shelter the universe. How immeasurably blessed am I—I who have been so long blinded by my pride of power and wealth ! Thou dost bestow thy mercy and grace upon me by accepting all that belonged to me, and in return thou givest thyself to me."

The Lord of the universe in the form of the dwarf said : " My devotee is glorified everywhere. Thou art my devotee, and thou art truthful. In earth and heaven art thou glorified for this gift of thine to me."

BOOK NINTH

THE ARGUMENT

THE Sūta continues to relate, after Śuka, the *Bhāgavatam*. Here are given two ancient legends : " The Story of King Ambarīsha " and " The Story of Rantideva."

CHAPTER I

THE STORY OF AMBARISHA

AMBARISHA became the monarch of the whole earth. All wealth and all enjoyments were at his command ; but these meant very little to him, for he loved the Lord, and he knew the vanity of earthly delights. Wealth and pleasure attract only the ignorant. He who has come to love God, the only eternal, blissful existence, knows that all else is but a vanishing dream.

Ambarīsha's mind was always fixed on Śrī Krişņa ; his tongue uttered only his praises ; his hands were engaged only in his service ; his ears heard only his Word ; his eyes saw everywhere the expressions of his divinity ; his sense of touch felt only his divine presence ; his sense of smell perceived only the fragrance of his holiness ; his sense of taste savoured only the food accepted by him : his feet walked only towards his Presense ; and his head touched his Lotus Feet.

He, the Lord, the Ātman, existeth everywhere and in all beings : knowing this, Ambarīsha offered all his labours to him as worship. Those who find the Lord of bliss manifest within their hearts are never attracted by vain earthly desires

Ambarīsha, thus unattached, reigned in his kingdom, his mind enjoying continuously the divine bliss. Once he made a vow to the supreme Lord of the universe, in observing which he practised special disciplines for one year and at the end of this time fasted for three days. On the fourth day he made gifts of his possessions to the poor and the needy, and then was about to break his fast when the sage Durvāsā approached him. The king made obeisance to him and invited him to partake of the feast. After accepting the invitation Durvāsā went to perform his ablutions in the sacred river Kālindi. There, his bathing finished, he became absorbed in meditation. Time passed. The king was anxiously waiting, for the auspicious period when he must break his fast was slipping away. He knew that if he did not break his fast within that period the performance of his vow would be of no avail. Yet to break his fast before the arrival of the invited guest was not becoming to a king. He therefore compromised by drinking water, which was in a sense breaking fast, but which at the same time did not involve an insult to his honoured guest.

When Durvāsā arrived at last and learned that the king had accepted drink during his absence, he was much disconcerted, for he felt that the king in his pride as monarch had wittingly slighted him. In the first heat of his anger he cursed the king. The curse took the form of a demon who approached King Ambarīsha to devour him ; the king, however, remained calm and unafraid, and this behaviour baffled the demon, rendering him impotent. Finding himself thus powerless with respect to the king, the monster turned around and advanced toward Durvāsā in order to devour the being from whom he had issued. Durvāsā sprang away in a desperate effort to save himself from his own curse, but found no way of escape. At last he went to Brahmā, and then to Śiva, but neither of them could help him, for in that curse he had wished to injure a devotee of Viṣṇu, the all-pervading Lord of the universe. In a final effort he approached Viṣṇu, who said :

"I also am powerless, for thou hast offended my devotee. I love my devotees, and I am a willing slave to my love. How can it be otherwise, since these devotees of mine willingly sacrifice everything for my sake ? They have surrendered themselves completely unto me. When anybody curses such a devotee, his curse with increased force, returns upon himself. One only can deliver him. Go to him whom thou hast offended by thy curse, and ask his forgiveness. This only can save thee. Go thou immediately, and I wish thee well."

Finding no other way to escape from his own curse, Durvāsā humbly approached Ambarīsha and begged his forgiveness. The king showed him due respect and readily forgave him. Then to counteract the curse and also to free Durvāsā from its effect upon himself, King Ambarīsha offered this prayer :

"O Lord, Thy infinite power existeth in all.
Thou art in the fire, Thou art in the sun,
Thou art in the moon, Thou art in the stars,
Thou art in the water, Thou art in the earth,
Thou art in the ether, Thou art in the wind,
Thou art in the subtle elements of the universe:
Thou art all in all.
Save and protect Durvāsā with Thy all-loving power.
May we all find Thy peace!"

Now Durvāsā found peace in his heart and was cleansed of all evil.

CHAPTER II

THE STORY OF RANTIDEVA[1]

In the glorious days of old India, when men loved to know the Lord and walk in his ways unceasingly, there lived a patriarch whose virtues were extolled in heaven and on earth. He was a king and had a large family and retinue, but it never occurred to him that they might ever come to want. For was it not true that all the necessities of life would be brought to his door if he trusted in the Lord and served

[1] The translation is that of Swāmi Sāradānanda, revised.

his fellow beings, looking upon them all as the veritable image of Hari, the Lord of the universe ? And, strangely enough, food, clothing, and all that he needed used to come to him, though he never toiled like other men. The king was quite satisfied with what he obtained by depending thus upon the Lord, and he shared his benefits with all around him. His hospitality was famous, for never would he say nay to anyone, however low his caste might be, who came to him for food or drink. The sympathy of the good king for all beings knew no bounds. He tried in every way to supply their wants and felt grieved when he had not the power to do so. Thus years rolled on, and the king was glad to think that the Lord Hari had made him the refuge of the destitute and the needy.

But there came a time when the king himself was in want and what he had was not enough for himself and his dependants. It was indeed a period of great trial for him, but he kept on relieving the distress of the poor, as formerly, and placed his entire confidence in the Lord. The scarcity grew worse, but he would not think of feeding himself and those that he called his own before he had satisfied the hunger of the poor who came for his help. Thus, many a day, the virtuous king had to go without food, but he was happy to think that by depriving himself he could serve his suffering fellow-beings.

The famine grew worse still, and there came a day when he found he had nothing to offer to the needy who came to his door, nor anything with which to feed himself and his family. Nothing came to him, even though at this time he rested his faith more than ever upon the Lord. And now he, with all his dependants, fasted day after day, but never did he relinquish his belief in the power and righteousness of Hari. Forty-eight days he had thus lived without any food or drink, when a pot of porridge, made of flour, milk and ghee, was brought to him. By that time the king and his people could hardly move, so much overcome were they by the hunger, thirst, and weakness of body occasioned by their fast.

Now just as they were about to take their meal, who should appear but a hungry Brahmin, much in need of food! The king, receiving him with respect as the image of Hari, gave him part of the porridge. When the Brahmin, satisfied, went away, immediately there came in a Śūdra, who also begged for food. The king straightway satisfied the Śūdra with a portion of the remainder of the porridge. Then entered a Chaṇdala, accompanied by dogs. From his wretched tale it appeared that he and his dogs had not had any food for many days. The king gave him a hearty welcome, and saluting him and his dogs as Hari, offered him the rest of the porridge. Now there was nothing left for the starving king and his family excepting a little drink. At this juncture a man of even a lower caste than a Chaṇḍāla entered and asked the king for a drink, as he was dying of thirst. The noble king, seeing him faint with thirst and exhaustion, addressed him in these gracious words : " I desire not of the Lord the greatness which comes by the attainment of the eight-fold powers, nor do I pray him that I may not be born again ; my one prayer to him is that I may feel the pain of others, as if I were residing within their bodies, and that I may have the power of relieving their pain and making them happy." So saying, the king gave the man the drink, and noted at once that his own fatigue, hunger, thirst, and the unrest and despondency of his mind, had all disappeared ; he had thus, by ministering to the wants of another, restored himself.

Now the rulers of the different spheres, who could shower wealth and power on those that worshipped them, and in particular the greatest of them all, Māyā—the creative principle of Viṣṇu, and the mistress of the universe—appeared before the devoted king and told him to worship them all, in order that he might attain the riches of this world and so become free forever from the wants from which he had been suffering so sorely. The king saluted them as the different forms of Hari, his only Beloved, but asked for nothing, since he had no desire for the things of the world, even though he had suffered from the want of them. He rested his heart on Hari, loving and worshipping him without any thought of selfish gain. Then Māyā, the queen of the world, finding him thus determined not to worship her for what she had offered, disappeared, together with her attendants, like a dream.

Through the great love which he had for his fellow beings, this noble king Rantideva became a Yogi and realized Hari, the one indivisible ocean of knowledge, existence and bliss, the Soul of all souls, knowing whom one attains to everlasting blessedness and becomes free from all wants and doubts. As a result of the exemplary life of this great king, his followers also devoted themselves to the worship of Nārāyaṇa, and ultimately they too became Yogis.

BOOK TENTH

THE ARGUMENT

THE Sūta continues to relate, after Śuka, the *Bhāgavatam*. Here begins the story of the life of Śrī Krișņa.

INTRODUCTION

Wonderful is the teacher, Śrī Krișņa;
Wonderful are his deeds.
Even the utterance of his holy name
Sanctifies him who speaks and him who hears.

When evil prevailed upon earth, when Truth had been forgotten and life had become a sinful burden to mankind, there went out a prayer to God entreating him to come down upon earth as a Saviour of humanity. The omniscient, omnipresent Lord knew the sufferings of mankind, and out of his great and all-consuming love for his children wished to lift the veil of ignorance which covered their sight—to be born as man in order to show them once more how to ascend toward himself.

CHAPTER I

THE BIRTH OF KRIṢṆA

KING KAMSA, the most powerful and tyrannical monarch of his time, had a sister whom he loved very tenderly. This beloved sister Devakī, was about to marry Vasudeva. As a token of his fraternal affection the king presented the newly married couple with many costly gifts, and declared that he himself would drive their carriage.

In due time he fulfilled this promise, and Devakī and Vasudeva were very happy at the thought of their singular good fortune in having as their driver the dreaded monarch of the surrounding territories. There were ovations and rejoicings as they drove along, and everywhere the people were filled with happiness.

All went well until, of a sudden, King Kamsa heard a voice from the void saying: " O thou foolish one, whom art thou driving so merrily ? Knowest thou not that the eighth issue of her womb shall be the cause of thy death ? "

At this the terrible Kamsa sprang from his seat. Drawing his sword he would have killed his sister then and there, had not Vasudeva interposed and prayed the king to spare the life of his newly married wife, reminding him that not Devakī but her eighth child would be the cause of his death, and promising, because of the king's fear, that each and every one of her children would be given over to Kamsa to deal with as he wished. Thus was King Kamsa pacified.

When in the course of time children were born to Vasudeva and Devakī, the parents fulfilled their promise to Kamsa, who, one after another, killed seven of their children as soon as they were born. This of course caused much grief to Vasudeva and Devakī but there was no way to escape from the hands of the tyrannical king.

When at last the time for the birth of the eighth child was approaching, Kamsa ordered Vasudeva and Devakī to be cast into prison. Accordingly, both of them were thrown into the same dungeon and bound with the same chain.

Being friendless and helpless, they were sorely troubled in their hearts. Their only consolation was in prayer to the almighty, all-loving God ; and so they both prayed earnestly from the depths of their hearts, imploring him to protect them and their child. While thus ardently praying, they fell into a swoon. In the gloom of that unconsciousness a light suddenly flashed ; and in that light the thick, dark cloud of misery vanished, and with it the accumulated sorrows of recent years. The sun of gladness and peace, the Lord of Love, appeared before them, healing the wounds in their hearts and cheering and exhilarating them with his benign smile. They were enveloped completely in his love; and presently they were more blissful still, for they heard him speak these sweet words:

"Father and mother, weep no more. I have come at last to your rescue and to the escape of all the good. Earth shall complain no longer. The days of the wicked are numbered. The wretched Kamsa shall die. Once again there will be peace and goodness on earth.

"Open your eyes and see me born as your child. Carry me, father, to the house of thy good friend King Nanda in Gokula. His wife, the Queen Yaśoda, has just now given birth to a daughter. Exchange me for that daughter. Bring her with thee to this dungeon, leaving me on the lap of Yaśoda, who will be sleeping at the time. Nothing shall bar my path."

So it came to pass that Krisṇa, who was to remove the bondage of humanity, was born in a prison cell belonging to the monarch Kamsa.

Devakī kissed the sweet face of her child, forgetting all danger, but Vasudeva remembered the instruction received in vision. He clasped the child to his bosom, and at the moment he was ready to leave the prison his chains were loosened and the gates of the prison cell were opened wide. He crossed the river Yamunā, and, encountering not the least opposition, he exchanged his son for the infant daughter of Yaśoda. Returning with the baby girl, he placed her on the lap of Devakī. The gates of the prison then closed, and he found himself once more in chains.

Early in the morning Kamsa heard of the birth of a female child, and at once came to the prison to see the baby. Vasudeva implored him to spare the life of the child because there could be no cause of danger in a girl. But Kamsa paid no heed to his request. He caught the feet of the tiny baby firmly in his hands, lifted it high in the air, and was about to dash it against a stone, when behold, the infant slipped from his fierce, demoniac grip and assuming high above him the beautiful form of the Divine Mother, looked down upon him, and said : "Wretch, dost thou think to avert the will of the Almighty ? Lo, thy destroyer is flourishing in Gokula." After these words she vanished, and King Kamsa trembled.

The same morning all the people of Gokula rejoiced when they learned of the birth of a son to their beloved King Nanda. And

Yaśoda, the queen mother, unaware of the exchange which had taken place, looked with joy on the sweet face of her son.

CHAPTER II

YASODA SEES THE UNIVERSE WITHIN THE MOUTH OF THE INFANT KRISNA

ONE day, when Krisna was still a little baby, some boys saw him eating mud. When his foster mother, Yaśoda, learned of it, she asked the baby to open his mouth. Krisna opened his tiny mouth, and, wonder of wonders! Yaśoda saw the whole universe—the earth, the heaven, the stars, the planets, the sun and the moon, and innumerable beings—within the mouth of Baby Krisna. For a moment Yaśoda was bewildered, thinking, "Is this a dream or an hallucination? Or is it a real vision, the vision of my little baby as God himself?" Soon she composed herself, and prayed thus to the Lord of Love:

"May thou who hast brought us into this world of Māyā, may thou who hast given me this sense and consciousness that I am Yaśoda, queen of Nanda, the mother of Krisna, bestow thy blessings upon us always."

Looking at her baby, she saw him smiling. Then she clasped him to her bosom and kissed him. Yaśoda saw him as her own little baby Krişṇa—him verily who was and is worshipped as the Brahman in Vedānta, as the universal Self in Yoga, and as the God of Love by devotees; and she found an indescribable joy and happiness in her heart whenever she looked upon him.

CHAPTER III

KRIṢṆA ALLOWS HIMSELF TO BE BOUND

ONCE, while Yaśoda was holding the baby Kriṣṇa on her lap, she set him down suddenly to attend to some milk that was boiling over on the oven. At this the child was much vexed. In his anger he broke a pot which contained curdled milk and then went to a dark corner of the room, taking some cheese with him. After eating a part of it himself and getting his little face besmeared with cheese crumbs, he bagan to feed a monkey. When his mother returned and saw him, she scolded him. As a punishment, she decided to tie him with a rope to a wooden mortar. But to her surprise the rope, although long enough, seemed too short. She took more rope, but still it was too short. Then she used all the ropes she could find, but still Krisṇa could not be tied. This greatly mystified Yaśoda. Krisṇa smiled within himself, but now, seeing that his mother was completely tired out and perplexed, he gently allowed himself to be bound.

He who has neither beginning, nor middle, nor end, who is all-pervading, infinite, and omnipotent, allowed himself to be bound by Yaśoda only because of her great love. He is the Lord omnipotent, the Lord of all beings, the controller of all ; yet he permits himself to be controlled by those who love him. Not by penance, nor by austerities, nor by study is he attained ; but those who love him with whole-souled devotion find him easily, for they are his chosen—they who have pure love in their hearts. Infinite though he is, he may be realized through love.

CHAPTER IV

KRISṆA MANIFESTS HIS DIVINITY TO BRAHMĀ

WHEN in time Krisṇa had become a well-grown youth, he used to go out with other shepherd boys of his own age to play and also to tend the cattle in the neighbouring pasture ground of Śrī Vrindāvana. While the cattle grazed in the pasture, the boys would play together.

Once after their usual play they sat down to partake of the lunch which they had brought with them. To their surprise they suddenly saw that the whole herd of cattle was missing. All the boys except Krișṇa were much troubled, but Krișṇa told them they were not to worry but to finish their lunch, and that in the meantime he would find the cattle.

Now Brahmā, the Creator, who had stolen the herd of cattle to test the divine power of Śrī Krișṇa, took this opportunity to steal the shepherd boys also, as soon as Krișṇa had left them to go in search of the cattle. Brahmā imprisoned the boys, together with the cattle, in a mountain cave, where by his divine power he kept them sleeping and unconscious.

Krișṇa searched everywhere for the cattle but could not find them. Then, disappointed, he came back, only to discover that the boys also were missing. Realizing that all this must be someone's mischievous trick, and being curious to know the truth of the matter, he soon found through meditation and divine insight, that it was all a gay prank of Brahmā to test his divinity. At this, Krișṇa smiled to himself, and thought it a good occasion to teach Brahmā a lesson. He therefore left the boys and cattle in the care of Brahmā, and out of himself created as many more boys and cattle, with the forms and characteristics of their originals. Then he returned home with his mind-born boys and cattle. The parents saw no change. The mothers as usual kissed their boys. The cattle were housed in their respective places.

Now, as before, Krișņa went out every day to the pasture with the mind-born boys and cattle and played in the fields. No change was noticed by anyone, except that the mothers felt a greater love for their sons. Before, they had loved Krișņa more than their own boys; but now they loved them all equally, and the very sight of their children gave them that highest bliss which comes only to him who realizes the presence of the blissful Self, or the God of Love. Truly has it been said, "None loves the children for the sake of children, but for the divine Self that is in the children." The mothers were not conscious that Krișņa had become their sons, but in their heart of hearts they felt his divinity within each child. Indeed Krișņa is the Soul of all souls, the Self of all selves, with whom all souls are eternally united. In reality it is

Krisṇa who has become all beings. He has become, indeed, the whole universe.

This play of Krisṇa in many forms continued for about a year. Then one day Brahmā came to visit Krisṇa. He was surprised to see all the shepherd boys and also the cattle, for he was sure that by his own divine Māyā they had been kept asleep and unconscious in the cave of the mountain. Brahmā pondered within himself; then suddenly a new vision opened up before him. Looking at all the boys and the cattle, he saw that they were all Krisṇa. He looked about him and saw Krisṇa in each form in the universe, Krisṇa in all beings and things. He saw Krisṇa as the light of all lights, the revealer of the whole universe, and knew that everything was He. He then lost his outer consciousness and, absorbed in the deepest contemplation, he found himself one with Krisṇa. Brahmā now realized that Krisṇa, the Lord of the universe who is One without a second, who is the divine Self in all beings, was playing his divine play in human form as Krisṇa the man. He realized Krisṇa as God, the Lord of the universe.

Brahmā then offered this prayer to Śrī Krisṇa :

"Lord, Thou art formless, infinite, blissful existence;
Yet Thou has assumed this form
To gladden the hearts of Thy devotees
And so shower Thy mercy upon them.
Thy form is indeed pure Sattva.

"Blessed indeed are those
Who art not concerned about philosophy, or doctrines,
But who live and follow Thy life-giving words;
For such pure ones alone find thee,
Who art beyond thought.

"O Thou infinite,
Thou art both personal and impersonal.
Incomprehensible is Thy true being—
Yet, again, comprehended and realized art Thou
By those who control their outgoing senses
And become absorbed in deepest contemplation of Thee.

"Thou art blissful, unfading, eternal.
Thou art the light of all lights,
Pure, absolute.
Those whose divine sight is clear
Find Thee within themselves:

Loosed are they from the wheel of birth
and death.

" As in darkness we fancy a rope to be a
snake,
So in ignorance do we mistake the all-
pervading Brahman for the world we
see ;
But as light dispels the darkness
And the rope is seen as a rope,
So with the rising of the sun of knowledge
The phantasmal world vanishes,
And Thou art revealed—the true Brahman.

" Thou art the Ātman, the divine Self ;
Not without do the wise seek Thee, but
within,
For Thou art present in the hearts of all.

" Knowledge brings freedom,
But the mere intellect gives no knowledge
of Thee
Those who devote themselves to Thy service
Come to know Thee through Thy grace:
May I be even the least of Thy devotees,
And may I devote my life to Thy service
alone !

" Blessed indeed are the shepherd boys
and girls,

For they love Thee as their very own,
Thee, the eternal, infinite Brahman.
They that serve Thee with whole-souled
devotion
Enjoy Thy bliss with their whole being.
The Vedas only tell of Thee ;
Thy devotees behold Thee.

" O Kriṣṇa, Thou art the friend of the
destitute.
Thou art unborn, eternal ;
Yet Thou hast assumed this human form
For the good of all,
That all may taste of Thy heavenly bliss.

" Attachment and delusion bind a man only
so long
As he fails to take shelter at Thy Lotus
Feet."

Thus singing the praises of Kriṣṇa, Brahmā
brought back the shepherd boys and the cattle.
Then Brahmā returned to his heaven, and
Kriṣṇa played with his friends.

CHAPTER V

KRIṢṆA AND THE SHEPHERDESSES

ŚRI Kriṣṇa is the embodiment of love. Love
is divine, and is expressed in many forms. To

Yaśoda, the God of Love was her own baby Krișṇa ; to the shepherd boys, Krișṇa was their beloved friend and playmate ; and to the shepherd girls, Krișṇa was their beloved friend, lover, and companion.

When Śrī Krișṇa played on his flute, the shepherd girls forgot everything ; unconscious even of their own bodies, they ran to him, drawn by his great love. Once Krișṇa, to test their devotion to him, said to them, " O ye pure ones, your duties must be first to your husbands and children. Go back to your homes and live in their service. You need not come to me. For if you only meditate on me you will gain salvation." But the shepherd girls replied, " O thou cruel lover, we desire to serve only thee ! Thou knowest the scriptural truths, and thou dost advise us to serve our husbands and children. So let it be : we shall abide by thy teaching. Since thou art in all, and art all, by serving thee we shall serve them also."

Krișṇa, who gives delight to all and who is blissful in his own being, divided himself into as many Krișṇas as there were shepherd girls, and danced and played with them. Each girl felt the divine presence and divine love of Śrī Krișṇa. Each felt herself the most blessed. Each one's love for Śrī Krișṇa was so absorbing that she felt herself one with Krișṇa —nay, knew herself to be Krișṇa.

Truly has it been said that those who meditate on the divine love of Śrī Krișṇa, and upon the sweet relationship between him and the shepherd girls, become free from lust and from sensuality.[1]

---

[1] Of the episode in the life of Sri Krishna recorded in this chapter, Swami Vivekananda has said :

"Ah, the most marvellous passage of his life, the most difficult to understand, which none ought to attempt to understand until he has become perfectly chaste and pure—that most marvellous expansion of love, allegorized and expressed in that beautiful play at Brindaban, which none can comprehend but he who has become mad with, and drunk deep of the cup of love ! Who can conceive the throes, of the love of the Gopis—the shepherd girls—the very ideal of love, love that wants nothing, love that even does not care for heaven, love that does not care for anything in this world or in the world to come ?

"The historian who records this marvellous love of the gopis is one who was born pure, the eternally pure Suka, the son of Vyasa. So long as there is selfishness in the heart, so long is love of God impossible ; it is nothing but shop-keeping.

"Oh for one, one kiss of those lips ! One who has been kissed by Thee—his thirst for Thee increases forever, all sorrows vanish, and he forgets love for everything else but for Thee and Thee alone." Ay, forget first the love of gold, and name and fame, and for this little trumpery world of ours. Then, only then, will you understand the love of Gopis, too holy to be attempted without giving up everything, too sacred to be conceived until the soul has become perfectly pure. People with ideas of sex, and of

CHAPTER VI

KRIṢṆA RESTORES LIFE TO THE DEAD SON OF HIS TEACHER

In due course of time the prophecy was fulfilled. The tyrannical Kamsa, the embodiment of evil on earth, was killed in an open fight with Kriṣṇa the God of Love, after which Kriṣṇa released his parents Vasudeva and Devaki from the prison of Kamsa. Their joy knew no bounds when they met their beloved child.

Although Kriṣṇa was the teacher of all teachers and the embodiment of all knowledge, he kept his knowledge hidden, for he

---

money, and of fame, bubbling up every minute in their hearts, daring to criticize or interpret the love of the Gopis!

"That is the very essence of the Krishna incarnation. Even the Gita, the great philosophy itself, does not compare with that madness, for in the Gita the disciple is taught slowly how to walk towards the goal, but there is the very ecstasy of enjoyment, the drunkenness of love, where disciples and teachers and teachings and books, and even the ideas of fear and God and heaven—all these have become one. Everthing else has been thrown away. What remains is the mad transport of love. In complete obliviousness to all else, the lover sees nothing in the world except that Krishna, and Krishna alone, for the face of every being has become a Krishna, and his own face looks like Krishna, and his own soul has become tinged with the Krishna colour... *That* indeed was the great Krishna."

had assumed human form and human ignorance to show humanity how to ascend towards God and how to unfold the infinite knowledge which is already within man. Accordingly Krișņa went to study with a teacher, Sāndīpani, with whom he lived the exemplary life of a disciple for some time practising all the disciplines of life faithfully, and revering and adoring his teacher. In a short time he mastered the Vedas and the various sciences. When he had finished his studies he humbly wished to make an offering of some gift to his teacher.

Now it happened that Sāndīpani and his wife were grieved at heart on account of the untimely death of their only son. Knowing the greatness of Krișņa and his divine power, they took this occasion to ask him to bring their son back to life. It is said that to please his teacher Krișņa went to the King of Death, and that, through Krișņa's intercession Sāndīpani's son was restored to life.

It is told, further, that when Devakī, mother of Krișņa, learned of the return of the teacher's son, she begged to have her sons who had been killed by Kamsa brought back to life. Krișņa by his divine power enabled his mother Devakī to see all her sons as living, although not on earth, and Devakī forgot all her sorrow. These sons, the brothers of Krişņa, later attained absolute freedom from life and death.

CHAPTER VII

KRISNA SENDS UDDHAVA TO GOKULA WITH A MESSAGE OF LOVE

AFTER completing his studies Krişņa returned to his parents at Mathura. It was necessary for him to live there to fulfil certain purposes of his life, though his soul longed for Gokula, where his foster parents lived, and where his heart was with his beloved friends, the shepherd boys and girls.

One day he called for a dearly loved friend and disciple Uddhava, and requested him to go to Gokula with a message of love. He said :

" Uddhava, please go to Gokula, console my foster parents, and give my love to the boys and girls. The shepherd girls know me as their very soul. They have renounced all earthly pleasures for my sake, and thus they will love me always. I bring my peace and infinite happiness to those who forsake all other pleasures for my sake. The shepherd girls love me more than anything else in this world, and they love me for love's sake only."

Uddhava, the beloved disciple, gladly under-
took to deliver the request of his master. At
dusk he reached Gokula, where he found the
shepherd boys and girls singing songs of
divine love for Śrī Kriṣṇa and recounting in
song his divine play and divine powers. Uddhava went directly to the home of Śrī Kriṣṇa.
There the foster parents, Nanda and Yaśoda,
were overjoyed to see one who was the friend
of their child. They welcomed him as their
own son and conversed with him, recounting
every detail of the childhood days of Kriṣṇa.

Uddhava·was thrilled within his heart and
said : " Thou, O Nanda, art indeed blessed,
for thou dost love Kriṣṇa, who is teacher of
the world. Blessed indeed are those who have
their mind and intelligence united with the
Lord of Love, for they shall become free from
all evil and shall reach the supreme goal.
Thou and thy wife are blessed in your love
for him, who is the cause of all causes, the
soul of all beings. Thou hast indeed overcome all Karmas.

" Grieve not for the physical absence of
Kriṣṇa. Though he is away, he is still near
you. As fire remains hidden in the wood, so
does he exist as the innermost Self in all
beings. To him all beings are equal. None
is hateful to him ; none is dearer to him than

others. Neither father, nor mother, nor wife, nor son, has he. Birthless, deathless, formless, is he. Nevertheless for the protection of the good, and for the establishment of Truth, doth he embody himself for his divine play on earth. Beyond all Guṇas is he; yet, associating himself with the Guṇas he is the creator, preserver, and destroyer of the universe.

"Śrī Krisṇa, the God of Love, who stealeth away the hearts of all, is not thy son alone. He is the son, he is the father, he is the mother, he is the friend, he is the Lord, of all beings in the universe. Nay, he is the Self of all. He is all. There is nothing beyond or above him."

Thus conversing on Śrī Krisṇa, they passed the night joyfully. Next morning Uddhava met all the shepherd girls, who gathered around him and inquired about their beloved Krisṇa. Uddhava said:

"How blessed are you to have surrendered yourselves completely and whole-heartedly to Bhagavān Śrī Krisṇa, the God of Love. Love and devotion grow after one has practised many austerities, undergone many spiritual disciplines, such as service, worship, concentration, and meditation. But fortunate indeed are you who were born with all-consuming love and devotion, and have renounced everything for the love of your dear Kriṣṇa. O happy ones, who enjoy the bliss of divine love, I am blessed and purified by coming into your presence.

"Bhagavān Śrī Kriṣṇa has sent this message to you all:

'I have never been separated from you, for I am your Self and I am the Self in all beings. You must realize that I am always with you.

'As the ocean is the end and goal of all rivers and streams, so am I the end, the supreme goal and purpose, of all the Vedas; of the eight-fold practices of Yoga; of discrimination, renunciation, performance of duties, and self-control.

'O ye who are so beautiful, my object in staying away from you is that ye may meditate on me and find me within your own hearts. So do I ask of you that ye control the restlessness of your minds and meditate on me, surrendering yourselves to me. Soon shall ye find me within yourselves and attain to my being. Even those who have not seen me and yet meditate on me, they also find me and attain to my being.'"

Greatly did the shepherd girls rejoice at this message from their beloved. Uddhava stayed in Gokula for some days, to the joy of all—

days that were spent in talk about Kriṣṇa and so passed all too rapidly away.

CHAPTER VIII

KRIṢṆA BY HIS DIVINE TOUCH GIVES KNOWLEDGE AND FREEDOM TO MUCHUKUNDA

MUCHUKUNDA, a retired king who once had much power and splendour, had renounced everything, and was now practising austerities and meditation in the cave of a mountain. His heart remained heavy, however, and his mind still groped in ignorance. Śrī Kriṣṇa, knowing of his sincere struggle for spiritual life and desiring to give him love and knowledge, entered the cave. Muchukunda was surprised to see the stranger, but realized at once that he was in the presence of a great soul in whose face shone the glory and splendour of God. Therefore he addressed him humbly : "Honoured master, I am Muchukunda, asleep to spiritual truths but fervently desiring the light. Who art thou ? Please tell me thy birth and deeds."

Śrī Kriṣṇa smilingly said :

"Many· are my births, and uncounted are my deeds, the great sages sing of them ; and they are never to be exhausted. But I will acquaint thee with my present birth and the deeds of this life.

"Brahmā and other gods prayed that I might come to destroy the wicked, to protect the good, and to re-establish the Truth. I was born the son of Vasudeva, and am known in this life as Vasudeva. I have already destroyed the wicked Kamsa and other vicious rulers.

"O thou kingly sage, I have come to thee to give thee of my wisdom. Thou didst pray long for me. I love my devotees and fulfil their dearest wish : having attained me, one has no more grief, for no longer has one any desire. But do thou ask for any boon, and I will grant it."

Muchukunda, knowing Krișṇa to be Nārāyaṇa himself, prostrated himself at his Feet and prayed :

"Lord, deluded by Thy Māyā
People know Thee not,
Nor do they worship Thee,
But remain attached to this world,
The source of sorrow and suffering.

"Some renounce the pleasure of life
And practise austerities,
Hoping to find greater pleasure in their
lives to come.

Thus attached to Karma and to fleeting things,
They never know Thy joy supreme.
" But when, O Lord, through Thy grace
A wandering, restless mind perceives the evanescence of worldly pleasure,
And seeks the company of holy men,
Then in that sacred companionship
There comes to it abiding love for Thee,
Thee who art the Lord of Love,
The supreme goal and final refuge of all.

" O Thou compassionate One,
Through Thy grace I have no yearning for enjoyment ;
No consciousness have I of a personal self.
My sole desire is to serve Thee ;
I seek no other boon.

" O Thou, Lord of all free souls,
Thou art the giver of freedom
What fool finding Thee would ask of Thee aught
Save attainment of Thy being and of Thy freedom ?
O Thou, the pure, without attributes, without form,
Supreme Brahman, the One without a second,
Renouncing all, I take refuge in Thee.

"O Thou, the refuge of all,
Long have I suffered from unquenchable desires;
Many a life have I wandered from birth to death,
And from death to birth.
Of peace have I found none;
Therefore do I take shelter at Thy Lotus Feet.
Those who seek refuge in Thee
Become free from fear, free from grief!
Verily they attain the Truth.
O Lord of the universe, I seek Thy freedom!"

Krişṇa by his divine touch gave Muchukunda freedom and knowledge, whereupon the king, with the joy and peace of God in his heart, went to Badarikāśrama in the Himālayas, there to live in divine contemplation of Brahman the Supreme.

CHAPTER IX

KRIṢṆA GIVES WEALTH TO A POOR BRAHMIN

ONCE there lived a learned Brahmin who was a friend of Krişṇa. He was a man of self-control, quiet and composed amid the opposites of life. He was very poor, but nevertheless contented, for his desires were few. His wife, however, was always complaining of their poverty. One day she said to him : " Krişņa is now the emperor of emperors. Immense wealth is at his command. Moreover, he is very kind-hearted and gives whatever is asked of him. Since he is your very dear friend, why do you not go and appeal to him ? He will surely give you enough to make us rich."

The Brahmin agreed to go to Krişņa, both for his own sake and to please his wife. He thought to himself, " I could not appeal to him for wealth, but this is a good opportunity to visit my loving friend, the divine Krişņa."

Then he said to his wife, " I must not go to him without some offering Please give me something to carry with me for my friend."

Whereupon she gave him a handful of flattened rice tied in a piece of cloth.

As the Brahmin entered the palace where Krişņa then lived, he felt within himself a perfect peace, and when Krişņa welcomed him as his beloved friend the Brahmin's joy knew no bounds.

After the Brahmin had rested, Krişņa holding his hand, they sat together and talked of the old days when they were studying together with the teacher Sāndīpani.

While they were thus conversing, Kriṣṇa suddenly asked the Brahmin, " Friend, what hast thou brought from home for me ? I am pleased to accept whatever is given me with love, be it ever so slight a thing — a leaf, or a flower, or a bit of fruit, or water."

Though Kriṣṇa gave him much encouragement, the Brahmin felt a little embarrassed to offer him the flattened rice which his wife had sent, and so remained silent.

Now Kriṣṇa, the omniscient Lord of the universe, knew the innermost heart of the Brahmin, knew that he did not love and worship God for the sake of wealth, knew that he loved him for love's sake only, and that he had come there out of kindness to his dear wife. And so, to please his devotee, Kriṣṇa thought to himself, " I will surprise him with vast riches." Then suddenly he snatched from his friend the little packet of flattened rice, and with great pleasure ate it, saying, " Ah, how good it is ! "

The Brahmin remained for the night as Kriṣṇa's guest and the next morning departed for home. There was, it is true, a little heaviness in his heart, for he did not know what he would tell his wife. She would surely be expecting him to bring much wealth. But how, he thought, could he have asked of

Krişņa any material thing? No, he was contented with his poverty and altogether happy in Krişņa love. Thinking thus, he walked slowly on.

Then, as he drew near his home, there came to pass a strange thing. Nowhere could he find his poor hut, but saw instead a vast palace in the midst of a beautiful garden. He rubbed his eyes to see if he were dreaming — but no, it was not a dream. Sweet music was in the air, and his wife, arrayed in lovely garments and costly jewels, with many maidens as her attendants, stood there to welcome him.

Then the Brahmin prayed, saying, "O Lord, may I not be attached to this wealth that thou hast given me. May I love thee always for love's sake only. May I be born again and again as thy friend, as thy servant; and always may I devote myself to thee."

BOOK ELEVENTH

THE ARGUMENT

THE Sūta continues to relate, after Śuka, the *Bhāgavatam*. This part concludes both the story of the life of Śrī Krişņa and the

Bhāgavatam proper. It consists mainly of the teachings of Śrī Krișṇa.

CHAPTER I

THE GODS' PRAYER TO ŚRĪ KRIṢṆA

BRAHMĀ and Śiva descended from their highest heavens with their attendants and other gods to pay homage to Śrī Krișṇa at Dwārakā. They knew that the Lord of the universe had assumed the form of Śrī Krișṇa, who, to the delight of all, was taking away the sins and impurities of all human beings by spreading the glory of righteousness and establishing Truth in the world. As they reached the beautiful city of Dwārakā, the city of splendours, and beheld Śrī Krișṇa, their hearts were captivated by the beauty of his youthful form and the radiant purity revealed in his features. They laid flowers gathered from the gardens of heaven at the Feet of the Lord and sang his praises :

"We praise Thee, O Lord, and surrender ourselves, heart and soul, at Thy Lotus Feet.

Thou dost deliver from the bondage of evil karma those who meditate upon Thee with the true fervour of devotion.

O Thou Lord invincible,
By Thy inscrutable divine power Thou hast brought forth this universe;
And having brought it forth, Thou dost reside within it;
Thou dost maintain the universe;
And then, unto Thee again, the universe goes back in dissolution.
But the universe does not limit Thee, nor do any action.
For Thou art unattached, shining in Thine own glory, immersed in the infinite bliss of the Self.
O worshipful Lord supreme,
If one has evil desires in his heart, what good can come to him from mere study of the Scriptures?
Neither charity, nor austerity, nor work can avail him aught.
But blessed indeed is he who, with heart purified, meditates on Thy glories;
His soul melts in joy when he hears of Thy splendour.

"Free us from bondage to evil!
May Thy Lotus Feet be like fire to consume our evil thoughts!
Thy Lotus Feet are meditated upon by the sages, whose hearts melt in love for Thee;

Thus do they realize happiness and become free from woes.
In diverse ways and forms Thy Feet alone are worshipped by those who seek union with Thee;
They worship Thy Feet to transcend even heaven itself.
"When the priests with folded palms pour oblations into the sacrificial fire, it is Thy Feet they worship;
And the Yogis, striving for union with Thee, desirous of knowing Thy divine power, meditate upon Thy Feet alone;
Thy Feet are worshipped in diverse ways by all the great lovers of God in every age and every clime.
Thou dost accept even the humblest offering of Thy most humble devotee.
May Thy Feet be like fire to consume our evil thoughts!
"O Thou Lord infinite,
May Thy Feet deliver us, Thy devotees, from all evil.
Thy Feet cover the whole universe;
The sacred river Ganges flows from them;
They put fear into those who are wicked and ungodly,
And they make fearless the good and the godly.

"Let Thy mercies fall upon us and protect
us;
May Thy Feet give us that which is good.
Thou art the supreme Being,
Beyond all limits of time and space,
The ruler and guide of all.

"Thou art the origin of this universe;
In Thee it has its being and continuance;
And verily unto Thee does it go back in
dissolution.
Thou art the ruler of that which is called
the undifferentiated;
And Thou art the guide of all earthly beings.
Thou art the intelligence of all intelligence.
Thou art Time, which we know to be of
immense power and all-destructive.
Thou art indeed the supreme.

"Thou art verily the infinite Brahman,
without form, without attributes;
Thou art also the father-mother God
omnipotent.
By Thee and within Thee is conceived the
universal intelligence
Whence issues this universe with all the
objects, subtle and gross;
Therefore art Thou the Lord of the sentient
and the insentient.

Thou, the Lord of the senses, though moving amongst objects of sense, dost remain unaffected by them.
Thou hast indeed shown us the ideal: to live in the world and yet not to be of it."

Brahmā and Śiva, with all the other gods, saluted the Lord, while they sang his praises, and ascending towards heaven said:

"Lord, we entreated thee to establish the kingdom of God on earth. Thou, who art the innermost Self of all, hast accomplished our desire. Thou hast established the Truth in the hearts of the godly and of those that are true seekers. Thy glory spreads in all directions, thy glory that dispels the mist of ignorance and impurity.

"Blessed indeed is the man who hears and recites thy deeds of unsurpassed valour, and who meditates upon thy divine play, for he shall transcend all ignorance.

"O Lord, thou supreme Being, a hundred years, yea more, have passed since thou camest to earth. Now, thou support of the universe, now hast thou fulfilled the mission of thy incarnation. Therefore, if it be thy desire, deign to return to thy eternal abode, to protect us and to guide us forevermore."

Then the blessed Lord, assenting, said:

"I have determined to leave the earth. My play here is finished. My kingdom is established."

Brahmā and Śiva, pleased at heart, saluted the Lord of the universe, and went back with all the other gods to their heavenly abode.

CHAPTER II

THE IDEAL OF RENUNCIATION

UDDHAVA, ever devoted to Śrī Krişṇa, learned of the master's intention to leave the earth and return to heavenly abode. Finding Śrī Krişṇa alone, he drew near, and prostrating himself at his Lotus Feet addressed him reverently :

O thou, God of gods,
Prince among Yogis,
Blessed are they who speak thy Word,
And Blessed is he who hears of thee.
Thou hast willed to leave this earth
And go to thine eternal abode.
Thou art the Lord of my heart, O Keśava ;
Separation from thee is intolerable even for a moment :

Take me with thee to thy dwelling place.

O Krişṇa, blessed indeed are they who but hear of thee and meditate on thy divine life and thy divine play, for they become free from all worldly desires and attain to thy being.

But how can we, thy devotees, thine inseparable companions, live apart from thee ?

Thou art our only beloved,

Thou art our very Self.

Verily, we thy servants will conquer thy Māyā, the delusion of existence, merely by living in thy holy company and by doing thee service.

Sages and saints there are, who, freed from physical consciousness, practising great austerities, living continent lives, self-controlled, pure, and free from worldly desires, attain thy being, the abode of Brahman ;

But we who live in the world, still attached to karmas, can overcome the world, by thy grace alone.

We can overcome this world, and go beyond the boundless ocean of darkness only by conversing of thee with thy devotees, by remembering thee and reciting thy deeds and words, by think-

ing and meditating on thy divine life
and thy divine play.

Śrī Krișṇa :

O blessed one, what thou hast heard is
true :
I wish to go back to my heavenly abode.
I have now fulfilled the mission for which
I was born.
O noble soul,
When I am gone, thou must renounce the
world.

Renounce attachment to friends and relatives, give up the sense of " me " and " mine ", wander everywhere with thy mind absorbed in me, seeing me in all.

Verily do I say to thee, this objective world, which is recognized by the mind and perceived by the senses, is only a projection of consciousness. It is transitory, and therefore not real.

Both good and evil exist in this world for the man who is not self-controlled and who through ignorance, sees the many. For him there are experiences of both good and bad karmas, as well as of inaction.

Therefore do thou control thy senses, and with thy heart purified behold the universe in the Self, and the Self in me, the supreme Lord.

When thou hast gained knowledge and wisdom and canst feel unity with all embodied beings, when thou dost know the Self and dost find delight in the Self, then art thou free from all limitation.

Thou shalt go beyond both good and evil. Good actions will proceed from thee without any thought of merit, and thou shalt desist from evil actions naturally and not through a sense of evil.

A friend to all poised, established in knowledge and wisdom, seeing me as the Self of the universe, verily shalt thou overcome grief and attain to freedom.

Uddhava :

O Lord of Yoga, O thou the treasure of the Yogis, the embodiment of Yoga, the very source of Yoga—thou hast recommended to me, for my highest good, the path of renunciation, known as Sanyāsa.

O thou Infinite, this renunciation of desires is difficult indeed for people attached to the world, but how much more difficult for those who have no devotion in their hearts for thee, who art the Self of all!

Dull am I of understanding, dwelling in the domain of Māyā, passionately attached to the ego and to the pleasure of the world: teach me, thy servant, O Lord, that I may faithfully follow and carry out thy words.

O Lord, thou art self-effulgent, the embodiment of Truth. Thou art the Ātman, the innermost Self in all beings. Thou art the teacher of teachers.

Weak and afflicted by worldliness am I. In thee I take refuge. O thou Lord of the universe, omniscient, the friend of man, teach me of thy wisdom.

Śrī Krisṇa

Men with discrimination free themselves from evil and worldliness by their own exertions.

Thy Self is thy true teacher. Verily by the Self alone is realized the highest good, first through reason, and then through direct transcendental perception.

The wise, who have attained inner poise, who are skilled in knowledge and Yoga, find me, with all my divine attributes and powers, most manifest in the human body.

Truly do I exist in all beings, but I am most manifest in man. The human heart is my favourite dwelling place.

When one has attained to birth and has developed self-control, he seeks to know me, who am found by transcending the senses.

Development of the power of introspection enables one to feel the reality of my existence. In illustration of this truth, O Uddhava, hear thou an ancient tale.

CHAPTER III

AVADHŪTA HAD TWENTY-FOUR TEACHERS

Śrī Kriṣṇa (*continuing*)

SEEING a wise young Avadhūta wandering about fearlessly, Yadu, who was versed in the Scriptures, said to him :

" O Brahmin, thou art indeed free from the consciousness of ego. Tell me, please, how didst thou attain thy vast wisdom, which enables thee to roam, free from care like a child, over the face of the earth ?

"Usually men seek religion and desire knowledge with the ulterior motive of gaining success, fame, and prosperity.

"But thou, who art shrewd, talented, learned, a most pleasing speaker, with many avenues to success open to thee, dost not work or make the least exertion for thine own good! It is as if thou wert an idiot.

"And yet while people are being scorched by the strong fire of lust and greed, thou dost remain untouched by its heat. O Brahmin, pray tell me how thou, though living a lonely life, dost find delight in thy Self alone, untouched by the miseries of the world?"

Being thus questioned by the intelligent Yadu, the noble Brahmin replied:

"O King, I roam on earth a free soul, having received wisdom from many teachers. Listen and hear who are my teachers: the earth, air, ether, water, fire, the moon, the sun, the pigeon, the python, the sea, the moth, the elephant, the bee, the honey-gatherer, the deer, the fish, the courtesan Pingalā, the osprey, the child, the maiden, the arrow-maker, the snake, the spider, and a particular insect known as Bhrāmara-kīta.

"These are the twenty-four teachers from whom I have learnt great lessons and have gathered my wisdom. I will recount my lessons and will tell thee from whom I have learned and how. Hearken, then, to my words.

"From *Earth* I have learned forbearance and the accomplishment of good for the sake of good. Never should a man of steady wisdom swerve from truth nor lose his poise, even when oppressed by others. A wise man should, like the trees and the mountains, yield good to all. His very birth must be to such an end.

"As the *Air* remains unaffected by good or bad odours, so a wise man, though moving amongst sense objects of diverse characters, should remain untouched by good or evil. Even though housed in an earthly body and subject to its limitations, a truly wise man, his consciousness fixed on the illimitable divine Self, remains quiet, equable, and unmoved.

"Like the all-pervading *Ether* is the Ātman, present in the animate and in the inanimate. Upon the Ātman, omnipresent, pure and free, the wise man, even though living in the body, having realized his unity with Brahman, never ceases to meditate.

"As ether remains unaffected by the clouds driven by the wind, so does a wise man remain untouched by the changing phenomena of the universe.

"Like *Water*, clear, soothing, sweet, and purifying, is the sage; and like water he purifies all who revere him and who seek his company.

"He shines with a divine glory, he is radiant with a heavenly lustre—he who has become fearless and self-controlled through the practice of Tapas. Though moving like *Fire* among material objects, he remains unaffected by the evils therein.

"His divine power remains hidden at times, but it becomes manifest before those who adore him, desiring the Truth. He accepts their offerings of worship, and in return, again like the all-consuming fire, he takes away their impurities, and their evil karmas of the past and of the future.

"As fire assumes the forms of burning objects, so hath the all-pervading Lord assumed the forms of beings and things.

"As the flames rise and fall but not the fire itself, so birth and death belong to the bodies but not to the Self.

"With the revolving of time, changes take place in the appearance of the *Moon*, though they do not in reality affect the moon. So do the changes such as birth and death pertain to the body and affect not the Ātman.

" Just as the *Sun*, though one, appears as many when reflected in many vessels of water, so does the one Ātman, reflected in many individuals, appear to be manifold.

" Once a *Pigeon* lived with its mate in a nest on the branch of a tree. They loved each other and dwelt in close companionship. In due season young ones were born to them, and the happy pair reared them tenderly. One day, while the parent birds were away in search of food, their young were captured in a trap by a fowler. When the pair returned, the mother dove was beside herself with grief, and though knowing that to do so would be sure death, she herself entered the trap. The poor male pigeon, overwhelmed by the plight of his family, now lost all prudence, tumbled at once into the same snare, and was killed. In like manner the miserable man whose senses are uncontrolled, who has no poise, who is tossed up and down by the currents of life, and who, without discrimination, is attached to family and to family possessions—ultimately such a one, with all that he has, comes to grief.

" Having attained human birth, which is an open gateway to Brahman, one who, like the pigeon, remains attached to the ties of the world is not fit to be called human. Pleasures of sense may be had in all lives : leave them, then, to the brutes! Never does the wise man yearn after them.

"Food comes of itself to the *Python*, and with what chance brings he is satisfied. So does the wise man remain satisfied with whatever food chance brings to him, be it well-cooked or ill-cooked, sumptuous or meagre. He struggles not for the mere maintenance of life, because all of his energy and skill are rightly applied to keeping his mind united with God, the supreme goal towards which life moves.

"Like the *Ocean* when it is calm and placid, the wise man is tranquil, poised, deep in knowledge. The brimful ocean overflows not, neither do the rivers dry up; similarly the wise man, his heart united with God, remains calm and unchanged amidst the opposites of life.

"The person of uncontrolled senses resists not carnal desire, strongest of worldly tempters, and thus falls into abysmal darkness as the *Moth* falls into the flame. The fool, his vision blinded, is attracted to the transitory and therefore illusory enjoyments of lust and gold, and, like the moth, is destroyed.

"Look not with lustful eyes upon any. One who is lustful is caught in a trap, like the *Elephant*, at the touch of the she-elephant. Shun like poison, therefore, all promiscuity.

"Like the *Bee*, gathering honey from different flowers the wise man accepts the essence of different Scriptures and sees only the good in all religions.

"Hoard not wealth as the bee hoards honey. One who does so is like the bee, who together with his wealth is destroyed.

"Be not as those who, like the *Honey-gatherer* stealing honey from the bee-hive, make a business of taking the hoarded wealth from the greedy and miserly, but who neither enjoy the wealth themselves nor permit any good to be done with it.

"The wise man should never listen to sensual music, but should take warning from the *Deer*, which, being enamoured of sweet sounds, falls into the snare.

"The ignorant and greedy man, whose organ of taste is not under control, meets with death like the *Fish* caught on a hook. The organ of taste is the most difficult organ to control. One who has control over it has control over all other organs.

"In days of yore there lived a courtesan named *Pingalā* in the city of Videha. I have learned a great lesson from her. Hearken, O King:

"One evening Pingalā, attractively dressed, stood as usual at her door to conduct any chance lover to the trysting place. She was passionately greedy for wealth, and as she watched men coming along the street, she cast her lustful eyes upon them, considering each a possible source of gain. For a long time they approached and passed by, one after another, untempted by her beauty. Nevertheless she fondly hoped that some rich man would yet come and lavish money upon her and she continued to watch at her door. Finally, long past midnight, tired and impatient, she felt within herself a deep disgust ; a clear light shone into her heart, and she saw her own folly.

" 'Alas for me !' she said to herself. 'How deluded have I been, how lacking in all self-control ! I have been indeed a fool to expect happiness from men.

" 'Near me is my God who is eternal, who is the true lover, in whom are delight and satisfaction, and in whom is all wealth. All the time has this wealth immeasurable been beside me. But I left my Lord, and like a fool I courted man, who can never satisfy my desires, who, on the other hand, causes misery, fear, disease, grief, and delusion.

" 'Oh, in vain have I afflicted my soul by this despicable mode of living ; in vain have I sought wealth and pleasure by selling my body to men who are themselves greedy slaves to lust. In this city of Videha I am perhaps the only foolish person, of wicked heart, who seeks enjoyment in such a gross, physical way.

" ' The Lord alone delighteth the heart. The unchangeable reality is he. He is the friend; he is the beloved; he is the master; nay, he is the very Self in all living beings. Renouncing the pleasures of the body, I will find my joy in him, and I will live in him for ever and ever.

" ' Objects of sense, which have a beginning and an end, can never give true enjoyment. Moreover, what woman ever found the highest good by depending on men, who are changeable and subject to death?

" ' Surely I have found the grace of the Lord, since out of disappointment has arisen in me this happy disgust. My misery has taught me the way to peace. Through the grace of the Lord I seek refuge in him alone and renounce the vain hope of finding gratification in the pleasures of sense. Through his grace I shall live content with whatever befalls me, and shall take delight only in the company of my beloved, the Lord of Love. He alone could save me, fallen as I was into the bottomless pit of evil and by my worldliness robbed of true vision.

"When one sees this universe as ephemeral, one gains true discrimination and turns away from worldliness. The Self becomes the Saviour of self.'

"Having gained this true discrimination, Pingalā gave up all vain hopes, composed herself, and attained peace and tranquillity.

"Hope is the cause of the greatest misery. Abandonment of hope is the highest bliss.

"Attachment," continued the Avadhūta, "leads to misery. Freedom from attachment brings endless joy. This is the lesson I have learned from an *Osprey*, who was attacked and followed by other and stronger birds as long as he carried a piece of flesh in his mouth. As soon as he gave up the piece of flesh he became free and was happy.

"Praise and blame are alike to me. I have no care, no anxiety, as those have who are attached to family and possessions. I find my playmate in the Lord, I take delight in the contemplation of the Self, and like a *Child*, unrestrained and happy, I wander about freely.

"The wise man, having passed beyond the Guṇas, is happy and free from care, like a little child—yet how unlike! For the child is happy through ignorance, the wise man through knowledge.

"I have learned a lesson from a *Maiden.* Hear this too from me.

"Once upon a time a young man, accompanied by his retinue, came to the home of a maiden to seek her hand in marriage. To prepare food for the guests, the girl found it necessary, her family being absent, to do the husking of the paddy herself. Now, because of her girlish pride she did not wish her love and his followers to find out that she was engaged in so menial a task, and as she husked the paddy the conch bracelets on her wrists made such a noise that she felt certain her occupation would be discovered. Being a clever girl she hastened to get rid of the jangling bracelets throwing them away one by one until only two were left on each arm. But as she went on husking, even these, striking together, broke the silence. She then removed one more bracelet from each arm. Now at last, from the single bracelet, there was no sound.

"This I have learned from her: Where many dwell in one place, there is noise, and quarrelling; even where there are only two people, there may be harmful gossip. Better it is, therefore, that one be solitary and alone, like the bracelet on either arm of the maiden.

"Seating oneself firmly, controlling the

breath, shaking off all lethargy, one should gather the scattered forces of the mind and practise concentration. Steadiness in concentration is attained by repeated practice and by keeping oneself free from attachment.

"The mind, when it is steady in divine contemplation, expresses Sattva overcoming Rajas and Tamas. No more is there feverish hankering after worldliness. Tranquillity comes to a heart which is no longer stirred by desires, as stillness to a fire when no more fuel is added.

"One with such a concentrated mind rises above the tumult of the subjective as well as of the objective world. He is like the *Arrow-maker*, who while fashioning his arrows is conscious only of his task.

"The *Snake* enters into a hole made by others, and there lives happily. What home can bind a sage? Wandering alone, he resorts to caves. He makes no show of his spiritual worth; and he is reticent of speech, for he speaks only words which are beneficial to others.

"As the *Spider* weaves its thread out of its own mouth, plays with it, and then withdraws it again into itself, so the eternal, unchangeable Lord, who is formless and attributeless, who is absolute knowledge, and absolute bliss, evolves the whole universe out of himself, plays with it, and again withdraws it into himself.

"As a man thinketh intently, whether through love, or hate, or fear, so doth he become. The cockroach, being attacked by a *Bhramara-kīta*, becomes a Bhramara-kīta: it thinks only of its foe, and as a result is transformed—without losing its original consciousness—into the object of its fear.

"All this have I learned from these many teachers. Now hear what my own *Body* has taught me.

"Reflecting on the nature of the body as subject to birth and death, and as the cause of suffering and misery, I have awakened within myself dispassion and discrimination. Knowing myself separate from the body, I have learned, with its help, to meditate on the eternal Truth.

"This body, for the sake of whose pleasure and comfort a man takes a wife, builds a home, holds possessions, and painfully accumulates wealth, withers and falls away like a tree.

"If they remain uncontrolled, the senses undermine—as does the possession of many wives—a man's moral nature.

"The Lord through his divine powers created various forms, such as trees, reptiles, beasts, birds, insects, and fish, but with these he was not content. Then he created the human form : this being the instrument best adapted for realizing him, God was pleased.

" Having achieved human birth, a rare and blessed incarnation, the wise man, leaving vain things to the vain, should strive to know God, and him only, before life passes into death.

" My worldliness dispelled, the divine light my guide, I roam over the earth free from attachment and egoism, firmly established in Self-knowledge.

" Verily can one learn the Truth from many teachers. Brahman, though One without a second, is named variously by the sages."

Thus taught by the Avadhūta, King Yadu also became free from attachment and attained to peace.

CHAPTER IV

KNOW THYSELF

Śrī Krisṇa : (*continuing*)

TAKE thy refuge in me and perform the duties of life without attachment.

Reflect with a purified mind on the evils of attachment.

This evanescent and myriad world perceived of the senses is as unfruitful as revery, as empty as a dream.

With thy mind fixed on me, engage thyself in selfless activity, which brings freedom. Give up selfish work, for it creates bondage. One devoted to the quest of Truth goes beyond duty.

With thy mind steadfast in me, practise the primary virtues, such as doing no injury, truthfulness, non-coveteousness, chastity; form regular habits of cleanliness, study, contentment and, with single-hearted devotion, surrender thyself to me.

Serve the Guru, thy teacher, who is tranquil, and who has realized me and has become one with me.

Shun all pride and jealousy. Give up all idea of "me" and "mine." Unite thyself with thy Guru by the strong bond of love. Use thy intelligence in eagerly seeking the Truth but be not impatient. Be free from envy, and give up all vain, unnecessary talk.

Learn to look with an equal eye upon all beings, seeing the one Self in all. Be not attached to thy wife, or thy children, or thy house, or thy possessions.

Thy Self, the Ātman, is the eternal witness, self-luminous, distinct from the physical or astral bodies, just as fire that burns and gives light is separate from the wood.

As fire appears to have small or great volume, and beginning and end, through being falsely identified with the burning wood, so does the Ātman appear to take on the attributes of the body by dwelling within it.

Verily, attachment to the body causes all bondage and misery. Know ye the truth of the Self, and be free.

Thou seest reality in the transitory body because of ignorance. Remove this ignorance that veils thy true knowledge, and know thy Self as pure, free, divine, absolute.

Knowledge is happiness. Let the fire of knowledge be kindled by following the path as revealed by a proficient teacher. Let the fire of knowledge remove the delusion which binds thee to the Guṇas and the working of the Guṇas. Then shalt thou attain peace and tranquillity.

As long as there is consciousness of diversity and not of unity in the Self, a man ignorantly thinks of himself as a separate being, as the "doer" of actions and the "experiencer" of effects. He remains subject to birth and death, knows happiness and misery, is bound by his own deeds, good or bad.

If a man has accomplished good deeds, he goes after death to higher spheres called the heavens, and there enjoys the effects of such deeds. But after the expiration of their effects he is again thrown back into the mortal world.

When, however, a man has performed evil deeds, his course is downward. He goes helplessly to various darker spheres, and, when returned to earth enters Tāmasika bodies. What mortal can expect eternal happiness through deeds which result in grief alone? Verily does the doer of such deeds remain subject to transmigration.

Actions are the play of the Guṇas. Man, uniting himself with the Guṇas, is the doer and experiencer. He imagines the one Self as manifold. Verily does he remain bound and dependent so long as he sees not the One but the many. When, however, he sees the one Self in all, he has freed himself from the Guṇas.

Those who make enjoyment the goal of life come to grief.

Uddhava :

Lord, pray tell me how one may become free, even while subject to the influence of the Guṇas. How may a free soul be distinguished from one in bondage? How does one who is free live and act? May it also please thee to remove this doubt of mine: "How is it possible that the soul, which is eternally free, should become bound?"

CHAPTER V

BONDAGE AND FREEDOM OF THE SOUL

Śrī Krişņa:

THE Self, eternally free, appears to be bound because of its association with the Guṇas. The Guṇas themselves being the product of Māyā, there is, in reality, no bondage of the soul.

Grief and delusion, happiness and misery, even the birth and death of a soul—all these things are the effects of Māyā. As a dream to a waking mind, which knows it to be a dream, so is the experience of birth and death to the eternal soul.

My Māyā has within itself the power to bind as well as the power to liberate. Avidyāmāyā causes apparent bondage to the soul. Vidyāmāyā banishes ignorance; and then the soul, which is my being, knows itself to be free.

Now I shall tell thee more of the Self in man and also of the difference between the bound and free soul.

Two birds of beautiful golden plumage, which look alike and are inseparable companions, have built their nests, of their free will, on the selfsame tree. One of them eats the sweet and bitter fruits of the tree, yet the other, which does not taste of its fruits at all, is greater in strength and glory. The one that does not taste of the fruit is indeed wise, and knows the Self from the non-Self ; but not so the other that tastes of the fruits. Associated with ignorance, the one remains bound, while the other, possessing knowledge, is eternally free.

The wise man, who is awakened from this dream of ignorance, even though living in the body, knows himself to be apart from it. The ignorant man, who is still dreaming dreams, identifies himself with the body.

The wise man, who looks upon himself as the unchangeable reality, though his senses move amongst material objects knows himself to be, not the doer, but the witness of the senses responding to their objects.

But the ignorant man, living in the body, which is but the result of his deeds in his previous lives, identifies himself with the deeds of the present life, the deeds which are but the play of the Guṇas. And thus does he become bound by his actions.

The wise man, who is free from attachment to the Guṇas and their workings, is not, like the ignorant man, bound by deeds. Even though living in the midst of the Guṇas, he remains pure and unaffected, like the clear sky above, or the self-luminous sun, or the all-cleansing fire. With doubts dispelled by the pure light of knowledge, he awakes from the dream of the manifold universe and sees the one Self in all beings. Free indeed is he from the limitations of the body, though living within it, if his heart be without attachment and without desire. He remains unaffected even though his body engages in actions and his mind in thoughts.

Truly wise is he who is unstirred by praise or blame, by love or hatred. He is not moved by the opposites of life. Verily does he delight in the blissful Self.

Unfruitful indeed is all labour, if one is merely versed in the Scriptures and does not realize and live the Truth.

These truly are the sources of misery : a cow that no longer yields milk, an unfaithful wife, physical slavery to another, a wicked son, wealth in the hands of the undeserving, and words which do not express God's truth.

Give up therefore all vain talk ; come out of the mire of delusion ; find tranquillity by fixing a purified mind upon me, the omnipresent Brahman. If, however, thou art unable to keep thy mind steadfast in me, engage thyself in work, without attachment, surrendering the fruits of such labour unto me.

O Uddhava, the many births that I have assumed and the deeds of my incarnations are sanctifying. They are for the good of all. Hear of them with reverence. Sing of my divine glory. Meditate on me ; and having me as thy supreme refuge, pursue duty, right desires, and wealth, for my sake alone. Thus shalt thou acquire unswerving love for me, who am the eternal Truth.

He who with love and devotion meditates on me—of a surety he compasses my being.

Uddhava :

Pray tell me, O Lord, what qualities in thy devotees and what kinds of devotion are most pleasing to thee.

Śrī Krisṇa :

My devotee is compassionate towards all beings ; he bears enmity towards none ; he is forbearing ; his only strength is Truth. Free from impurities, he looks with an equal eye upon all beings, and works for the good of all. His heart is unsullied by desires; self-controlled, sweet-tempered, pure, free from the consciousness of ego, serene, temperate, a master of his mind, having me as his refuge, he meditates on me steadily. Imperturbable, tranquil, patient, having the whole of nature under his control, he seeks not honour for himself but gives honour to all.

Completely enlightened himself, such a sage can convey the Truth to others. He is friendly and merciful to all beings. He knows good from evil, and by surrendering his actions unto me, he worships me alone.

Those who, knowing my true nature, worship me steadfastly are the first among my devotees. Worship me in the symbols and images which remind thee of me, and also in the hearts of my devotees, where I am most manifest. Take delight in hearing and reading of my divine incarnations.

Observe the forms and rituals as set forth in the Scriptures, without losing sight of their inner spirit. Take special vows of devotion to me, and be initiated according to the Vedic or other scriptural rites. Offer unto me that which is very dear to thee—which thou holdest most covetable. Infinite are the results of such an offering!

Meditate on me, surrendering thyself to my service.

Trumpet not thine own good deeds. Shun egotism, and avoid hankering for name or fame. Use not the light of knowledge for selfish ends.

The sun, fire, knowers of Truth, a devotee, ether, air, water, earth, the body, and all creatures—these are the objects, the symbols, wherein to worship me.

Worship me in the sun through Vedic hymns.

Worship me in the fire through oblations, saying to thyself that all thy impurities are therewith consumed.

Worship me in the knowers of Truth through hospitality and service.

Worship me in the devotee by welcoming him cordially.

Worship me through meditation in the sanctuary of the heart.

Worship me in the air by seeing it as divine energy, and in water by accepting it as the symbol of divine purity.

Worship me in the earth by repeating the sacred Mantram, my holy name; worship me in the body by offering it food and drink: and worship me, the indwelling spirit in all beings, with an even constancy of vision.

In all these abodes worship me, in my benign form, thy chosen ideal; and worship me with a concentrated mind.

He who thus worships me through work and meditation lives continuously in me and attains unswerving love for me.

O Uddhava, of all the paths to me, who am the goal of the sages, the path of love is the happiest and best!

Now shall I tell thee the profound secret of this path, for thou art my disciple, my companion, and my friend.

CHAPTER VI

THE SOCIETY OF THE HOLY

Śrī Kriṣṇa (*continuing*):

SPIRITUAL discrimination, virtuous deeds, sacrifices, study, austerity, repetition of the sacred Mantrams, resort to places of pilgrimage, righteous conduct—all these are aids to spiritual unfoldment; but the greatest help is the society of the holy, for by serving the saints and associating with them one cuts asunder the roots of ignorance and attachment. Many have attained the highest illumination, not by the study of the Vedas, nor yet by the practice of austerities, but merely by loving and serving the men of God.

Therefore, O Uddhava, laying aside the formalities of religion, do thou wholeheartedly take refuge in me, the Self of all beings, and so pass beyond fear.

Uddhava :

O thou prince of Yogis, though I am listening to thy words, the doubts that disturb me are not dispelled, and hence my mind is not steadfast.

Śrī Krișņa :

O Uddhava, this whole universe exists in me and is an expression of my divine power. I am the infinite, undifferentiated, immutable Lord, One without a second. This apparent, manifold universe is an expression of my power.

The tree of transmigration is ancient, growing upon Brahman as its soil. It is rooted in thirst for life, in innumerable desires. The Guņas are its trunks, the gross elements are its boughs, the senses and the mind are its leaves and twigs. Material objects are its sap, happiness and misery its fruits. (Vultures—worldly people—eat the fruit of misery ; swans—people with discrimination—eat the fruit of happiness.) Though seemingly solid and eternal, the tree is unreal as a mirage, and evanescent as a dream. In the light of the one and only Truth, the transcendent Self, it vanishes and is gone.

Therefore, steady and watchful, thine axe of knowledge sharpened by associating with the holy, and by serving the Guru with single-hearted devotion,[1] do thou cut down the tree of transmigration, know thy Self and Brahman as one, and attain forever to freedom.

CHAPTER VII

DIVINE SONG OF HAMSA OR THE SWAN

Śrī Krisṇa (*continuing*):

THE three Guṇas—Sattwa, Rajas, and Tamas—belong to the mind and not to the Self. Rise thou above the Guṇas and know the Self. First, overcome Rajas and Tamas by developing Sattwa, and then rise above Sattwa by Sattwa itself.

When Sattwa is developed, a man attains true love for me and steadfast devotion to me.

[1] Literally, " one pointed devotion "—devotion in the highest degree concentrated, focussed. The same epithet is used to describe a mind in a state of religious meditation.

There is a predominance of one or another of the Guṇas in things, objects, and persons. Our deeds and our thoughts express one or another of them. Indeed, every object in the manifold universe is informed with either Sattwa, Rajas, or Tamas. To develop Sattwa, associate only with those who already express Sattwa. Thence will arise devotion, which is purifying ; then will follow illumination ; and finally will be achieved the highest good — freedom.

Uddhava :

O Krisna, men are generally aware of the ephemeral nature of sense pleasures, and they know them to cause suffering and misery ; yet how is it that they run after them indiscriminately, like the beasts of the field ?

Śrī Krisna :

The ignorant man knows not the Self, and has not the peace and tranquillity which arise from such knowledge. He identifies himself with his body, mind, and senses, and is overcome by desires of the flesh. As he comes into contact with objects of enjoyment, he dwells on thoughts of pleasure. Dwelling on thoughts of pleasure, he loses the power to discriminate and becomes attached to the senses.

Under the sway of strong impulse the man who is devoid of self-control wilfully commits deeds that he knows to be fraught with future misery. But the man of discrimination, even though moved by desires, at once becomes conscious of the evil that is in them, and does not yield to their influence but remains unattached. He controls his mind and dwells steadfastly on divine thoughts.

Give up lethargy ; practise concentration on me regularly : withdraw the mind from everything else and become absorbed in me. This process of Yoga, O Uddhava, has been taught by Sanaka and by others of my disciples.

Uddhava :

O Kriṣṇa, I pray, tell me when and how Sanaka and others learned Yoga from thee.

Śrī Kriṣṇa :

Sanaka and other spiritual sons of Brahmā approached their father with the object of learning the profound secret of Yoga, and asked him, saying : " Revered sir, the mind is drawn towards objects of sense, and these attach themselves to the mind. How can one, seeking liberation, free himself from the clutches of attachment ? " To this question

Brahmā found no answer. Then he meditated upon me, and I appeared before them all in the form of a swan.

Being eager to know the Truth, they asked, "Who art thou?" and in the form of the swan I replied:

"O sages, if thy inquiry is concerning me, the Self, then thy inquiry is useless; for there is but one Self. If thou dost refer to the body, there is unity in matter also, everything being composed of the same elements; and, again, therefore, thy inquiry is meaningless.

"Verily is the mind drawn to objects of sense, and the objects attach themselves to the mind. But thou art neither the mind nor the sense objects. Thou art ever one with me, thy Self. Give up false identification of thyself with the mind or with the objects which act and react upon one another, and know thy Self as one with me. Give up false ego, for that is the source of all misery.

"Even though apparently awake, one is still asleep if one sees multiplicity. Wake up from this dream of ignorance and see the one Self. The Self alone is real.

"Thou art the Self, the eternal witness. Drive away the ignorance of attachment by the light of knowledge kindled by pure reason, true discrimination, and direct perception of the Self; and worship me who am seated in the shrine of the heart.

"This world to-day is, to-morrow is not—empty as a dream, shifting like a circle of fire. There is but one consciousness—pure, transcendental—though it appears as multiple in form.

"Withdraw thy mind from the objective world. Give up thirst for life, and becoming tranquil-minded be absorbed in the divine bliss.

"After thou hast experienced the divine bliss, this objective world will no more lead thee into error, for thou wilt know its appearance to be illusory.

"The man who has realized his true Self and attained perfection, though his senses may move among objects, is not affected by them, nor does he ever identify himself with body or mind.

"Having attained samādhi and having realized the Truth, he no longer attaches the Self to the non-Self.

"O sages, this is the profound secret of Sāmkhya and Yoga.

"Know me to be the supreme goal, the end of Yoga and Sāmkhya, the end of truth, valour, glory and self-control.

" Practising the ideal of non-attachment and seeing the unity of the Self, in all, worship me, who am thy beloved friend, thy Self."

This is the secret of Yoga, which, while I was in the form of a swan, I taught to Sanaka and to others.

CHAPTER VIII

BHAKTI YOGA

Uddhava (*addressing Śrī Krisṇa*):

VARIOUS ways of attaining the highest good have been taught by various teachers. Thou dost teach the path of devotion. Are all of these ways equally good?

Śrī Krisṇa :

I revealed my wisdom first to Brahmā in the form of the Vedas. Brahmā declared that wisdom unto his son Manu, from whom the seven patriarchs and sages—Bhrigu and the others—received it. From them it passed on to their sons and disciples, who, being of various temperaments and natures, understood it variously. Thus arose the several interpretations of the Vedas.

Many are the means described for the attainment of the highest good, such as love, performance of duty, self-control, truthfulness, sacrifices, gifts, austerity, charity, vows, observance of moral precepts. I could name more: But of all I could name, verily love is the highest: love and devotion that make one forgetful of everything else, love that unites the lover with me. What ineffable joys does one find through love of me, the blissful Self! Once that joy is realized, all earthly pleasures fade into nothingness.

To the man who finds delight in me alone, who is self-controlled and even-minded, having no longing in his heart but for me, the whole universe is full of bliss. Neither the position of Brahmā nor that of Indra, neither dominion over the whole world, nor occult power, nor even salvation, is desired by the devotee who has surrendered himself unto me and who finds bliss in me.

Such a devotee is very dear to me.

Noble indeed is he, unsmitten by desires, calm, compassionate towards all—the man who is devoted to me. He alone knows my infinite bliss; and his happiness is unconditional. Even though not yet master of his senses, my devotee is never completely overcome by them; his devotion to me is his particular saving grace.

As fire kindled into a blaze burns the faggots to ashes, so, O Uddhava, devotion to me completely consumes all evil.

Neither by Yoga, nor by philosophy, nor by deeds, nor by study, nor by austerity, nor even by renunciation of desires, am I easily attained. Those only who have pure love for me find me easily. I, the Self, dear to the devotee, am attainable by love and devotion. Devotion to me purifies even the lowliest of the low.

Without love for me virtues and learning are unfruitful.

He who loves me is made pure ; his heart melts in joy. He rises to transcendental consciousness by the rousing of his higher emotional nature. Tears of joy flow from his eyes ; his hair stands on ends ;[1] his heart melts in love. The bliss in that state is so intense that forgetful of himself and his surroundings he sometimes weeps profusely, or laughs, or sings, or dances ; such a devotee is a purifying influence upon the whole universe.

---

[1] To the mystic in India this phenomenon, associated by the Westerner only with the emotion of great fear, is familiar as a physical expression of the extreme ecstasy caused by the highest spiritual emotion.

As gold smelted by fire gives up its dross and becomes pure, so all evil is charmed away from my devotee by the power of my love. He verily attains to me. Blessed are those who take delight in hearing or reciting the story of my divine incarnations, for their minds become pure. Blessed are the pure in mind, for unto them is given the wisdom of God.

By thinking of objects of sense one becomes attached to them. By meditating on me, and dwelling on thoughts of me, one experiences increasing love for me and at last is merged in me.

Let not thy mind run after the things of this world, for they are empty as dreams. Give thy mind to me, devote thyself to me, meditate on me.

Avoid promiscuity ; avoid even the society of the lustful. No other association causes so much grief and bondage as that with lustful men and women.. Learn to love solitude, and, ever alert, think of me without ceasing.

Uddhava :

O Lotus-eyed Krișņa, please teach me how to meditate.

Śrī Krişņa :

Sitting in an easy posture, with the body erect, place thy hands on thy lap and direct thine eyes towards the tip of thy nose. Practise Prāņāyāma—inhalation, retention, and exhalation of the breath—for the purification of the nerves. Next, practise gathering in the outgoing senses and the mind with great patience and perseverance.

While practising Prāņāyāma, meditate on the sacred word *Om*, chanted within like the continuous peal of a bell. You should practise Prāņāyāma, thus coupled with *Om*, ten times thrice daily. If you do this, you will quickly gain control of the Prāņa.[2]

Imagine a lotus within the heart, its petals pointing downward, and, running through it, the Sushumnā. As you meditate, think that the petals have turned upward, and that the flower is full-blown. Then see—at the heart of the flower—sun, moon, and fire, one within the other.

Then, your mind intent, behold within the fire the benign form of your Ishṭam. Meditate on him as the Supreme Cause, in whom the

---

[2] Before undertaking the practices of Prāņāyāma and meditation, one should learn the processes in detail from a competent teacher.

whole universe exists and from whom the whole universe evolves.

Then, last of all, meditate on the oneness of the Self with God, the one blissful existence, the one *I Am.*

With mind thus absorbed, a man sees me alone in himself; and sees himself in me, the Self of all—light joined to light.

A Yogi, thus practising meditation regularly, with intense devotion, soon rises above all limitations of knowledge and action by realizing the one, all-pervading reality.

CHAPTER IX

YOGA POWERS

Śrī Krişņa (*continuing*):

VARIOUS are the occult powers that come to the Yogi while practising concentration. These are the power of becoming larger or smaller or exceedingly light in weight, the power of obtaining everything one wishes, irresistible will power, the power to read minds, the power to live without food or drink, the powers of clairaudience, clairvoyance, levitation, the power of entering into another's body and many more. No power is beyond the reach of the sage who, self-controlled, poised, and tranquil has complete command of the Prāṇa, and who concentrates on me.

But great powers though these may be, they are regarded as obstacles by the true Yogi, who seeks union with me.

I am the Lord of all powers. I am the goal of all Yoga. I am the end of all knowledge. I am the Truth of religion, and I am the teacher of all teachers.

I am the Self dwelling in the hearts of all.

CHAPTER X

I AM THE ALL

Uddhava (*addressing Śrī Kriṣṇa*):

THOU art, in very truth, the supreme Brahman, without beginning and without end. Free art thou from all limitations. In thee exists the whole universe.

The ignorant know thee not, thou who dwellest in all beings, high and low. The wise know thee and worship thee in thy true being. Teach me, O Lord, how to worship thee in all beings and attain to thy perfection.

O thou, the supreme cause of the universe, thou dwellest hidden in all beings as the innermost Self of all. Deluded by Māyā, most men do not see thee, but all that is thou seest.

O thou of wondrous powers, tell me where thou art most manifest. Where is thy power greatly present, amongst beings and things both in heaven and on earth, in the nether regions, and in all quarters else?

Śrī Krisṇa:

O Uddhava, this same question was asked by Arjuna on the eve of the battle of Kurukshetra.[1] I will tell thee in brief my divine manifestations.

I am the Self in all beings, their friend and benefactor. I am the God of all. I am the supreme cause of their life and death. I am the All.

Of all that is moving, I am the motion. Of virtues I am even-mindedness. Of all attributes I am the primary attribute.

The life-principle am I of the living, the universal intelligence of the intellect. Of all things subtle I am the soul; and of things difficult to subdue I am the mind.

I am Brahmā, the teacher of the Vedas. Among sacred words I am the *Om*, consisting of the sounds A, U, M.

Of the great seers I am Bhrigu. Of kingly sages I am Manu. Of the divine seers I am Nārada. Of the great perfected souls I am Kapila.

---

[1] The reference is to the Gītā, Chapter X.

Of the progeny of Diti I am Prahlāda. Of satellites I am the moon.

Of all luminaries I am the sun, and of men I am the king.

Of metals I am gold. Of all controllers I am Yama, the king of death. Of the orders of life I am the monastic order, and of castes I am the Brahmin.

Of sacred rivers I am the Ganges ; of waters I am the ocean. Of weapons I am the bow, and of wielders of the bow I am Siva.

Of all abodes I am Mount Meru, and of inaccessible places I am the Himālayas. Of trees I am Aśvattha, and of grain I am barley.

Of priests I am Vasiṣtha, and of knowers of Brahman I am Brihaspati. Of generals I am Skanda, and of pioneers I am Brahmā.

Of sacrifices I am the study of the Vedas. Of vows I am the vow to injure none. Of purifiers I am the Self.

Of spiritual disciplines I am perfect control and perfect concentration of mind, and of victory I am the victor. Of intellectual power I am discrimination between the Self and the non-Self.

I am Śatarūpa among women, and I am Manu among men. Of saints I am Nārāyaṇa, and of celibates I am Sanatkumāra.

Of religious vows I am the monastic vow, and of the sources of well-being I am introspection. Of secrets I am the truthful word, and silence ; of seasons I am the spring.

Of the knowers of the Vedas I am Vyāsa, and of the wise I am Śukra.

Of the Lords I am Vāsudeva, and of devotees I am thyself.

Of gems I am the sapphire, and of things beautiful I am the lotus bud. Of species of grass I am sacred Kuśa, and of oblations I am the clarified butter.

Know that I am the energy and tenacity of the strong, and the devotion of the devout.

I am of water the sweet taste. Of resplendence I am the sun. I am the lustre of sun, moon, and stars ; I am the music of the spheres.

I am verily the origin, maintenance, and dissolution of all beings. I constitute the function of all the organs. Earth, air, ether, water, fire, the ego, cosmic intelligence ; all modifications of Prakriti ; Purusha and Prakriti ; Sattva, Rajas, and Tamas—I am all these. I am the supreme Brahman. I am knowledge and realization. Nothing whatsoever exists without me or beyond me.

The atoms of the universe may be counted, but not so my manifestations ; for eternally I create innumerable worlds.

Wherever there is power, beauty, fame prosperity, modesty, sacrifice, concord, fortune, strength, fortitude, or knowledge—there am I manifested.

I am revealed in those who are pure in heart.

Therefore control thy speech, control the restlessness of thy mind. Control also the Prāṇa, and the senses. And finally, control thyself by thy Self. Thus shalt thou overcome the world and give expression to me. As for the monk who has not fully controlled his speech, mind and intellect—his vows, austerities, and charity leak out like water from an unbaked jar.

Therefore, steadfastly devoted to me, gain control over speech, mind, and Prāṇa. To him who is endowed with love for me, O Uddhava, belongs the fullness of life.

CHAPTER XI

CASTES AND ORDERS OF LIFE

Uddhava :

O Krişṇa, thou dost tell of devotion to God ; but teach me how one may show that devotion even while attending to the daily duties of life.

Teach me also the duties of the classes and orders of life.

Śrī Krișṇa :

In the beginning, in the golden age, men had but one caste, known as Hamsa. All were equally endowed with knowledge, all were born knowers of Truth ; and since this was so the age was called Krita, which is to say, " Attained."

In that primeval age, OM was the Veda ; and I was duty, in the aspects of austerity, purity, charity and truthfulness. Men were pure, and were given to divine contemplation. It was their pleasure to meditate constantly on me—the pure, the absolute.

Next, in the silver age, there came a division of men into classes : some there were who pursued knowledge, others who pursued duty.

From the mouth of my universal form originated the Brahmin ; from my arms, the Kshatriya ; from my thighs and feet, respectively, the Vaiśya and the Śūdra. They were differentiated by their varied temperaments and by their specialized duties.

Family life sprang from my thighs, the life of the student from my heart, the life of retirement from my chest, and the life of the monk from my head.

Self-control, meditation, purity, contentment, forbearance, straightforwardness, compassion, truthfulness, devotion to me—these are the characteristics of a Brahmin.

Strength, patience, valour, fortitude, liberality, enterprise, steadiness, leadership, devotion to Brahmins—all these qualities belong to the indomitable spirit of a Kshatriya.

Faith, charity, service, and also a desire to amass wealth—these are the characteristics of a Vaiśya.

Service, humility, obedience, and a desire to follow in the footsteps of the great—these are the virtues of a Śūdra.

Uncleanliness, falsehood, theft, atheism, vain argumentation, incontinence, anger, and greed—these undesirable traits characterize a fifth class, beyond the pale of the other four.

Avoidance of injury to all beings, love of truthfulness and chastity, abhorrence of stealing, refraining from anger and greed, striving to be of service to all beings—these are the universal duties of all castes.

A man is called Dvija, or twice-born, when he receives his birth from above—the second birth—during the sacred thread ceremony.[1]

---

[1] Hindu ceremony of baptism or initiation, in which is taught the sacred Gāyatrīmantra—the meditation on the supreme Brahman.

Then he begins his student life, living in close association with a competent teacher. He must practise self-control, and he must study the Vedas. He should observe strict continence, never consciously departing from it. If he should become involuntarily impure, he should bathe, and after practising Prāṇāyāma repeat the Gāyatrī. Every morning and evening, after attending to cleanliness, he should silently chant the Gāyatrīmantra, meditating on its meaning with a concentrated mind. He must learn to offer his heart's worship to the divine Self in all beings and to see the one God residing in all.

He should look upon his Guru as God. Verily is the Guru the embodiment of divinity. Accordingly the student must serve him and please him in every way.

Bathing, prayer, and meditation, practised regularly—morning, noon, and evening; straightforwardness; the visiting of holy places; repetition of the sacred Mantram, while meditating upon all beings as myself; control of mind, speech, and body; these are the universal observances meant for all orders of life.

After completing the life of the student, one may enter upon either the family life, the hermit's life, or the monk's life.

CHAPTER XIV

SELF-CONTROL

Śrī Krișņa (*continuing*)

THOSE who do not follow the Yogas of love, knowledge, or work, as taught by me, but pursue instead the path of the worldly and seek to gratify their selfish desires through their restless senses—verily do those tread the round of birth and death.

One must be pure in heart to enter into the life of the spirit and follow the Yogas. To achieve purity of heart one must observe cleanliness, practise austerities, be compassionate towards all beings, and perform the appropriate duties of life. Work becomes consecrated and purifying when it is done as service unto me.

Detach yourself from the objects of desire. Abstain from worldly pleasures that you may thus free yourself from the entanglement of the senses. This is the righteous conduct that leads one to the highest good, and frees man from grief, infatuation, and fear.

By attributing worth to tangible objects, man becomes attracted to them ; attraction to them brings desire for them : desire leads to competition and dispute amongst men. These rouse violent anger, and the result is delusion.

One wishing to lead the life of a householder should marry a pure girl, who must be younger than himself. Always must he remember that the ideal good is not enjoyment but the attainment of Knowledge in this life and of everlasting happiness hereafter. As travellers meet by chance on the way, so does a man meet wife, children, relatives, and friends : let him therefore be in the world and yet separate from it.

After living a householder's life, one must enter into the hermit's life, or the life of retirement, preparatory to the life of renunciation. To the man about to renounce the world the Devas offer many obstructions, hoping that his effort to transcend them and to attain to Brahman will come to naught.

Verily he who speaks noble truths, and gives utterance to the Word of God, observes the vow of silence. Silence is restraint of speech.

Calm of spirit is achieved when one engages in action without selfish attachment. Such action results in poise and in perfect control of the body.

One who has learned the control of Prāṇa has self-control. One who has not this control, O Uddhava, does not become a monk, though he may wear the garb. A monk has his senses under perfect command. His delight is altogether in the divine Self. He is steady and tranquil, and looks with an equal eye upon all.

His mind purified because of his love for me, the sage should meditate on the divine Self as one with me. In his search for knowledge, he should reflect on the freedom of the Self and also on the cause of its bondage. Restlessness of the mind and the senses is the cause of bondage ; in the control of this restlessness is freedom. Therefore the sage should intently think upon me and become absorbed in love for me, for thus alone can he acquire self-control. When he turns away from the desire for pleasure, he finds infinite bliss in the Self.

The world of the senses has no absolute reality, for it perishes. Therefore a sage should give up desire for ephemeral enjoyments and live in the world completely unattached.

The Self alone is real. The world of the senses is super-imposed upon it. See the one reality, the divine Self, and so liberate yourself from thinking about the world of the senses. He who knows the one reality, beyond the objective world, has true knowledge. He loves me for the sake of love and does not care even for his own salvation. Such a free soul is above all rules of conduct and beyond all orders of life. Though wise, he is childlike. Though subtle, learned, and well-versed in the Scriptures, he wanders about as one who knows nothing. He causes no fear to anyone, and he is fearful of none. If vilified, he does not return the insult but remains calm. He bears enmity towards none.

The one supreme Self dwelleth in the hearts of all beings. That one existence is seen as many beings, just as the moon appears to be many when reflected in many vessels.

The wise man regards the body as only an instrument through the help of which, by meditating on the Truth and knowing the one existence, he may become free. The delusion of many existences is removed from the man who has realized me. He sees the One in the many.

Selfish attachment to the world of plurality leaves only pain in its wake. Be dispassionate, and, gaining self-control, approach the knower of Truth humbly and inquire into the truth that leads to me. A knower of Brahman is indeed one with me. Serve thy teacher with care and devotion.

Religion is not in the garb of a monk, neither in external forms. Control of the passions, a well-balanced mind, discrimination, and renunciation—these make one a knower of Truth.

Service unto the teacher is the duty of a student : protection of all living creatures, and sacrifice unto God—these are the duties of a householder ; duties of a hermit consist of practising austerities and learning discrimination ; and the duties of a monk are self-control and doing injury to none.

The practice of continence except for the purpose of procreation, the performance of the regular obligations of life—these, with purity, contentment, and kindness to animals, are also the duties of a householder.

The duty of all is to worship me. He who worships me constantly and steadfastly through the performance of his duties, knowing me as the supreme goal—such a one becomes endowed with knowledge and realization, and soon attains to my being.

All duties, if accompanied by devotion to me, lead to the supreme good and to eternal liberation.

CHAPTER XII

I AM THE GOAL, I AM THE WAY

Śrī Krisṇa : (*continuing*)

ONE who has not merely studied the Scriptures but has realized in himself the experience recorded in them, and has known the truth of the Self, sees the universe as illusory. He surrenders his knowledge, as well as the way to knowledge, unto me.

For I am the goal of the wise man, and I am the way. I am his prosperity. I am his heaven. There is nothing dearer to him than I.

He who is endowed with knowledge, O Uddhava, and with realization, has attained my supreme abode. I am the eye in all his seeing : thus it is that he knows me. Because he knows me, therefore is he dear to me.

Nothing is there more purifying than knowledge. Neither the practice of austerity, nor resort to places of pilgrimage, nor repetition of Mantrams, nor charity, nor any other spiritual discipline, can add to the perfection already attained through knowledge.

Therefore, O Uddhava, let thy knowledge be of thy Self, and endowed with knowledge and with realization worship me lovingly.

I am the sacrifice, and I am the Lord of sacrifice. The wise sacrifice unto me in their own selves through the offering of knowledge and of realization, and they attain to perfection, which is in me.

Thou art the Self, illimitable, unchangeable. Birth and death belong to the sheaths of the body, the gross, the subtle, and the causal—which in reality have no existence. Thou art beyond all these; therefore, O Uddhava, shouldst thou know thyself.

Uddhava:

Beloved master, teach me how to acquire this pure, ancient knowledge which thou dost speak of as dispassion and realization. Also teach me that love to which the great ones aspire.

When a man is visited by afflictions, blessed Lord, and is suffering torment in the labyrinthine ways of the world, I see no other refuge for him than the shelter of thy Feet, which shed blessed immortality.

Śrī Kriṣṇa:

O Uddhava, I consider him wise who sees the one Self in this manifold universe.

There is one absolute existence. On its surface appear the myriad forms of the phenomenal world like bubbles on the ocean. For a while they stay, and then they disappear. The one absolute existence, the abiding reality remains.

The Scriptures, direct experience, authority, and inference—these are the four proofs of knowledge. Finding through all these proofs the reality of the one absolute existence, the wise man is no longer attached to transitory things. The fleeting objects of this world become to him visions and dreams.

All happiness in the objective world ends in misery. The wise do not seek happiness either here or hereafter, realizing its evanescence.

Now, O Uddhava, I shall tell thee of the philosophy of love.

Drink deep of my words, which are nectar. Study the lives and teachings of my divine incarnations, the sons of God. Learn to find joy in my worship. Sing my praises.

Being devoted to my service, worship me with thy whole soul. Ennobling also is the service to my devotees. Learn to see me in all beings.

Let all thy work be done as service unto me. With thine every word extol my divine attributes. Free thy mind from all selfish desires and offer it unto me.

Renounce all enjoyments and pleasures; make sacrifices, offer gifts, chant my name, undertake vows, and practise austerities. Do all these things for my sake alone.

Thus by surrendering thyself unto me through all thy actions, and remembering me constantly, thou shalt come to love me. When thou hast come to love me, there will be nothing more for thee to achieve.

For when the mind is completely surrendered unto me, who am the divine Self within, the heart becomes pure and tranquil, and one attains to Truth, knowledge, dispassion, and divine power. Devoid of these is one whose mind is outgoing, seeking pleasure in objects of sense.

Truth is love. Knowledge is seeing the oneness of the Self with God. Dispassion is non-attachment to objects of sense, and divine power is the control of nature, external and internal.

The first requisites for spiritual life are these : doing no injury, truthfulness, honesty, non-attachment, modesty, abstention from wealth, faith in an after-life, continence, silence, patience, forgiveness, fearlessness, physical and mental purity, chanting the name of the Lord, austerity, sacrifice, self-reliance, hospitality, surrendering of the self to me, pilgrimages, working for the good of others, and service to the teacher.

These are known in Yoga as the practices of Yama and Niyama. These, my friend, if rightly followed, bring great spiritual unfoldment.

Calmness is a steady flow of the mind toward God.

Self-restraint is control of the organs of sense.

Patience is bearing the burden of life cheerfully.

Steadiness is overcoming the palate and the impulse of sex.

The highest charity is refraining from violence.

Austerity is the giving up of desire.

Valour is the conquest of one's own self.

To know the Truth is to see the oneness of the Self with God.

Truthfulness is true and agreeable speech as exemplified by the sages.

Purity is non-attachment to work.

Renunciation is overcoming the world.

Virtue is the treasure which men covet.

I, the supreme Lord, am the sacrifice.

The greatest gift is the gift of knowledge.

The greatest strength is the control of Prāṇa.

Fortunate is he who meditates on my divine powers.

The highest profit is in devotion to me.

Wisdom is the removal of false ideas of multiplicity and realizing the unity of the Self.

Modesty is abhorrence of evil deeds.

Excellence of character arises from disregard of worldly considerations.

Happiness is the transcending of both pleasure and pain.

Misery is hankering after pleasures of sense.

Learned is he who discriminates between bondage and freedom.

Ignorant is he who identifies himself with the body.

The right path is that which leads to me.

The wrong path is that which causes restlessness of the mind.

Heaven is the domination of Sattwa in the mind.

Hell is the predominance of Tamas.

The teacher who has realized his oneness with me is the true friend.

He indeed is rich who is rich in virtues.

Poor is he who is discontented.

Mean is he who is not master of his senses.

Godly is he who is not attached to objects of sense.

Divine is he who has overcome both good and evil.

CHAPTER XIII

THE YOGAS OF LOVE, KNOWLEDGE, AND WORK

Śrī Kriṣṇa (*continuing*):

THE Yogas of love, knowledge, and work have been given by me to men for their highest good. Except through these there is no way to attain freedom.

Of these, the Yoga of knowledge is for those who desire nothing; for they, knowing every desire to be fraught with evil, have renounced work. Those who still have desires, and who are attached to work, must follow the Yoga of work. The Yoga of love is successfully followed by those blessed mortals who take delight in me and in my Word.

Work one must, until the heart has become tranquil and free from desires. Work must be performed until one has come to love me and to take delight in my Word.

By doing one's duties for the sake of duty and performing them as services unto me, having no selfish end in view, one becomes free from both the good and evil effects of work. The Yoga of work frees the mind from all evil tendencies and purifies the heart. In the pure heart arise true wisdom and true love for me.

Blessed is human birth ; even the dwellers in heaven desire this birth ; for true wisdom and pure love may be attained only by man.

Seek not for life on earth or in heaven. Thirst for life is delusion. Knowing life to be transitory, wake up from this dream of ignorance and strive to attain knowledge and freedom before death shall claim thee. The purpose of this mortal life is to reach the shore of immortality by conquering both life and death.

Seeing that the tree on which it has built its nest is being felled by cruel hands, the bird gives up all attachment, flies away from its nest, and seeks elsewhere its well-being. Similarly, knowing that the tree of mortal existence is cut short by time, with its rotation of days and nights, the wise man gives up the thirst for life and realizes the supreme Lord. Thus does he free himself from the bondage of Karma and so find peace.

Rare indeed is this human birth. The human body is like a boat, the first and foremost use of which is to carry us across the ocean of life and death to the shore of immortality. The Guru is the skilful helmsman ; divine grace is the favourable wind. If with such means as these man does not strive to cross the ocean of life and death, he is indeed spiritually dead.

When the Yogi, seeing evil in all human undertakings, frees himself from attachment and worldly desires, he should with his senses under perfect control, practise holding his mind steady in meditation on the Ātman, the divine Self. If the mind wanders restlessly while he is practising meditation, he should take still firmer hold on it and patiently try to control its vagaries. He must never lose sight of the course of the mind, but watch the thoughts that pass through it. With the Prāṇa and the senses under control, and with purified intelligence, let him bring the mind under subjection.

The control of the mind is said to be the highest Yoga ; it is like the control of an unruly horse which must be made to obey its rider.

Attain discrimination and consider the universe as ephemeral. Reflect how all beings and things are subject to birth, growth, decay, and death — how fleeting are all. Having reflected thus, leave vain things to the vain, and gain tranquillity of mind. The man whose mind is tranquil, and who is unattached to the world, meditates on the Ātman as taught by the Guru, and becomes free from false ego.

Union with God, the Soul of all souls, is the end to be sought. Meditate on him either through the path of Yoga, which teaches self-control and concentration, or through the path of philosophy and discrimination, or through the path of worship and meditation. Besides these there is no way.

If the Yogi, being deluded, makes mistakes in life, he should burn away his sins and impurities by prayer and meditation. This Yoga of prayer and meditation is the only way of atonement.

If a man has acquired faith, takes delight in contemplation of me, is indifferent to work, and yet, though knowing their vanity, fails to give up all desires—let him with complete devotion continue to worship me with a cheerful heart. Though he may find it necessary to satisfy his desires, which he is unable for the time to give up, let him all the while ponder on the emptiness of such gratification and know it to be fraught with evil consequences.

One who thus worships me steadfastly with devotion soon attains purity of heart and finds me dwelling within. When he realizes me, the Self of all, the knots of his heart are loosened, all doubts cease, and he is free from the bondage of Karma. For the Yogi who loves me and whose heart is one with mine, there remains nothing to be attained.

Whatever is acquired through work, austerity, knowledge, detachment, Yoga or charity, or through any other means of discipline, can be attained easily by my disciple through love of me and devotion to me. Heavenly enjoyment, liberation, my dwelling place—all are within his easy reach, should he care to have them.

But of such nature are the great sages, those who are poised and who are devoted to me and love me for love's sake, that even though I offer salvation to them they do not desire it.

Desirelessness is said to be the highest good. Blessed therefore is he who has no desire.

Good and evil karmas bind not the great souls who are poised, who are steadfastly devoted to me, and who have realized the Self by reaching beyond the plane of mind and intellect.

Those who follow my teachings to the attainment of my being dwell in my blissful state, which is unity with Brahman.

Delusion completely overcomes man's sense of right and wrong.

O noble soul, when a man loses the sense of right and wrong, he lives in vain. For he lives steeped in dense darkness and misses the purpose of life. Engrossed in things of the world, knowing neither himself nor the supreme Self, he becomes an automaton and knows not what he does.

Verily is the universe come out of me, and I dwell in the hearts of all beings. But deluded souls, who are steeped in worldliness and seek only to gratify their senses, know me not. Blinded are they by the fog of ignorance.

CHAPTER XV

IMMORTALITY OF THE SOUL

Uddhava : (*addressing Śrī Krișṇa*)

VARIOUS are the doctrines of God, the soul, and the universe propounded by the sages. Pray tell me why the Truth is expressed in many ways.

Śrī Krișṇa :

Truth has many aspects. Infinite Truth has infinite expressions. Though the sages speak in diverse ways, they express one and the same Truth.

Ignorant is he who says, "What I say and know is true ; others are wrong." It is because of this attitude of the ignorant that there have been doubts and misunderstandings about God. This attitude it is that causes dispute amongst men. But all doubts vanish when one gains self-control and attains tranquillity by realizing the heart of Truth. Thereupon dispute, too, is at an end.

Baseless is the dispute as to whether the Ātman is or is not. Doubt is ignorance, and it never ceases for men who turn their faces away from God and who never meditate on me, the Ātman.

The Ātman is the indwelling Self in man, the reality in him. Not conscious of this Self within him, he identifies himself with his mind and senses, and so treads the round of birth and death, going from one sphere to another.

At the moment of death the sum of all the experiences of life on earth comes to the surface of the mind—for in the mind are stored all impressions of past deeds—and the dying man then becomes absorbed in these experiences. Then comes complete loss of memory. Next there arises before man's mind the vision of his life to come, a vision regulated by his impressions of his past deeds; and he no longer recollects his life on earth. This complete forgetfulness of his past identity is death.

His complete acceptance of another state and identification with a new body is said to be his birth. He no longer remembers his past life, and, though he has existed before, he considers himself newly born.

Like the flame of a lamp or the current of a river, the bodies of creatures, with the imperceptible passing of time, are in constant motion. Hence they are in a sense continually born and continually dying. Is the flame of the lamp one and the same now as before? Is the current of water one and the same always? Is man, if identified with the body, the same man to-day that he was yesterday?

Verily is there neither birth nor death to the real man; he is immortal. All else is delusion.

Conception, embryonic state, birth, childhood, boyhood, youth, middle age, and death—these are different states of the body and affect not the real man. But man, because of his attachment to the Guṇas, identifies himself ignorantly with these desirable or undesirable states, which belong of a surety to the body and not to the Self. A few, however, who are wise, who have attained knowledge, give up this identification and find eternal life.

The Ātman is the eternal witness, distinct from the body—as distinct as is the observer from the plant he watches shoot up from a seed, blossom into maturity, and die.

The ignorant man fails to know and experience the Self as distinct from Prakriti, and deluded by his attachment to the Guṇas of Prakriti goes from birth to death, from death to birth.

His next birth is regulated by his deeds of the present life—the deeds which make up his character. If his character is dominated by Sattwa, he achieves a higher birth, that of a Deva or of a Sage ; if by Rajas, he is returned to earth as an Asura or as a man ; and if by Tamas, he is born from the lower wombs.

The Guṇas belong to the mind. The Ātman, though birthless and deathless, appears to be influenced by the Guṇas and is seemingly born or meets apparently with death ; just as trees reflected on a stream of water seem to be moving with the stream, or as when the body whirls, the ground too appears to be whirling.

Indeed, birth and death and all the experiences of life are to the Ātman the experiences of a prolonged dream. Miseries, though belonging to the world of dreams, are of a certainty painful, and do not vanish until we cease our dreaming. Nor does this dream of life come to an end for him whose thoughts are engrossed in transitory, sensuous things.

Therefore, O Uddhava, control the outgoing senses. Restrain thyself. Learn to meditate upon the Ātman. When thou knowest thyself one with God, this dream will cease.

If thou dost desire the highest good, thou must have poise. Maintain thy equanimity even if placed in dire extremities. Let not thy peace be disturbed even if thou art ridiculed or ill-spoken of by others. Never return hatred for hatred, nor injury for injury. Desiring thy highest good, thou must strive to free thyself from evil and ignorance.

Uddhava :

O thou Soul of the universe, it is indeed difficult to maintain poise and peace within, when one is ridiculed, insulted, or unjustly spoken of by others. Kindly instruct me that I may have strength to follow thy path.

CHAPTER XVI

THE SONG OF THE MENDICANT

Śrī Krisṇa (*continuing*):

DIFFICULT is it indeed to maintain inner poise when pierced by the harsh words of the wicked. Arrows penetrating the most vital parts of a man's body do not cause so sharp a pain.

I will tell you a story of a mendicant, O Uddhava, who was maltreated by the wicked but who bore all insults patiently :

Once there lived in Avantī a Brahmin who was exceedingly rich and yet very greedy, miserly, and grasping. Never did he welcome any guest or friend, or relative, with even a kind word. Although his wife, his children, and his servants felt sorry for him, yet they despised him. He hoarded his money, and never used it to do any good to his friends or relatives or to give himself the slightest comfort.

Suddenly he lost all his hoarded wealth. He was penniless. As he reflected on his condition he found himself choking with sobs of remorse. He now saw clearly the vanity and evanescence of earthly treasure.

He said to himself : "Woe is me. I have vainly wasted my life in a mad quest for riches, which all too seldom bring happiness to man. Greed does not cease with the possession of wealth ; and the man of wealth lives in constant fear and anxiety lest he may lose it.

"Theft, cruelty, falsehood, ostentation, lust, anger, pride, haughtiness, dissension, enmity, distrust, competition, and the three indulgences—sex, wine, and gambling—these fifteen evils are said to be the outcome of wealth.

"Even kith and kin turn into foes for an insignificant sum of money.

"Having obtained this human birth, which is the gateway to Brahman and liberation—this birth which even the gods covet—those who, attached to lust and gold, disregard the summons of the Infinite, fail to realize the supreme good and inevitably meet with an evil end.

"The strength and energy that are wasted by the ignorant in search of vain and unrewarding wealth will lead, if wisely directed, to the door of freedom.

"Why is it that even so-called wise men suffer from time to time from greed? Surely the world must be utterly deluded by some inscrutable power!

"The Lord Hari, who is the embodiment of all divine qualities, must indeed be favourable towards me, for he has made me weary of the world—a condition which serves like a boat wherewith the struggling soul may cross the ocean of life and death.

"Therefore during the remaining years of my life I shall practise austerities and steadfastly devote all my energies to spiritual practices—those practices which, conducive to the highest good, will teach me to find joy in meditation on the Self alone.

"May the gods, who rule the three worlds, bless me."

Resolving thus in his mind, the good Brahmin of Avantī succeeded in loosening the knots of his heart and became a mendicant, calm and tranquil.

With his mind, senses, and Prāṇas under control, he wandered alone over the face of the earth, entering towns and villages only to procure his food, and none knew who he was.

Seeing the aged, shabby-looking monk, wicked people insulted him with various indignities and in many ways injured him bodily.

But maintaining his inner poise he silently bore all physical and mental wounds, and in spite of all obstacles steadfastly followed the path of good. Constantly wronged and tormented, he sang to himself this song :

"Nothing ever causes me pleasure or pain : neither the gods, nor the Ātman, nor any planet, nor deeds, nor the passage of time.

"Mind, the Scriptures declare, is the only cause of suffering. It is the mind that sets in motion the wheel of birth and death.

"Mind creates the modifications of the Guṇas, whence proceed the varieties of deeds characterized as white, black, or red. Our next birth and life are guided by the nature of these deeds.

"The Self, immersed in its own glory, though in close association with the mind, remains unaffected by the modifications of the Guṇas. The Self is the Lord, and the ruler; it is the witness of all thought. Upon it is reflected, as in a mirror, experience of the world. But man, by identifying himself with the mind and its modifications, attempts to satisfy his desires, and straightway he becomes bound.

"Charity, the performance of one's duty, the observance of moral and religious practices, and of vows, and the acquiring of merit—all these have one end, namely self-control. The highest Yoga is the control of the mind.

"Of what use are charity and other observances to one whose mind is under control and is tranquil? Of what use again, are charity and other observances to one whose mind lapses into dullness and who does not attempt to control it?

"All the gods are under the sway of the mind, but the mind never comes under the rule of any power.[1] Even the Yogis know

---

[1] According to the mythology of the Hindus each sense and sense-organ has a presiding deity. The 'gods' are these presiding deities, as well as the senses and sense-organs themselves.

the mind to be a terrible god, stronger than the strongest. He, therefore, who can bring the mind under subjection is indeed the god of gods.

"The uncontrolled mind is verily the invincible foe, whose onset is unbearable and whose weapon pierces the very vitals. There are some, very foolish and ignorant, who, without struggling to conquer this foe engage themselves vainly in fighting external persons and influences, and thus make men either friendly to them, or hostile, or indifferent.

"These blind, foolish people, who accept the body (which is but a creation of the mind) as 'me' and 'mine', ignorantly think, 'I am so and so, and this other man is different,' and hence wander in a limitless wilderness of perplexity and gloom.

"Even if thou dost think another person is causing thee happiness or misery, thou art really neither happy nor wretched, for thou art the Ātman, the changeless spirit; thy sense of happiness and misery is due to a false identification of thy Self with the body, which alone is subject to changes. The Self is the real Self in all. With whom shouldst thou be angry for causing pain if accidentally thou dost bite thy tongue with thy teeth?

"If thou dost think the gods are causing suffering, reflect that thou art not concerned with any suffering, for thou art the Ātman, the changeless spirit. All changes pertain to the senses, which alone are affected. With whom shouldst thou be angry if in thine own body one limb strikes another limb?[1]

"If the Ātman is regarded as the cause of happiness and misery, then no blame is attached to anyone, for the Ātman, in that case, must be expressing its own inherent nature. But the Ātman, which is existence, knowledge, and bliss, can have no other inherent nature or attribute. If there appear to be such, it is illusory. Hence there is neither pleasure nor pain. With whom, then, should one be angry?

"If the planets be the cause of happiness and misery, what has the Ātman, which is birthless, to do with them? The planets can influence that which is born, and may act upon one another, but the Ātman is different both from a planet and from that which is born. With whom, then, should one be angry?

---

1 Suppose the hand strikes the mouth, or the mouth bites the hand: the act concerns only their respective deities, Agni and Indra. The Ātman remains untouched. Suppose the hand of one person strikes the mouth of another: the situation remains the same, inasmuch as the presiding deity in each organ is identical in all bodies. (Substantially, from the commentary of Srīdharaswāmi).

"If deeds be regarded as the cause of happiness and misery, how can they affect the Ātman? Deeds affect the doer. The Ātman is not the doer, for the Ātman is self-sufficient. Therefore deeds, the supposed cause of pleasure and pain, can never affect the Ātman. With whom, then, should one be angry?

"Can it be that the progress of time causes happiness and misery? Even then the Ātman remains unaffected, for time exists only in the mind. Surely the flame of the fire is not affected by heat, nor ice by cold. So with whom should one be angry?

"Verily in the Ātman there is no relativity, no pleasure or pain, and indeed no opposites of any kind. Nor can the Ātman, which is beyond the Guṇas, be affected in any way by any cause whatsoever. It is the apparent self, the ego, which conjures up relative existence. The illumined soul is fearless, for he is untouched by the changes of mind and matter.

"So must I practise devotion to the supreme Self, the refuge of the great sages of old. Verily shall I cross the limitless wilderness of ignorance by worshipping the Feet of the Lord of Love."

This was the song sung by that sage, who, though vilified and insulted by the wicked, kept his poise and swerved not from the Truth.

There is no cause for the pleasures and pains of life outside of ourselves. It is the deluded mind that gives rise to happiness or misery. Friends and foes and those who are neither friends nor foes, nay this whole relative existence—all is a creation of the ignorant mind.

Therefore, my beloved, with thy intellect absorbed in me, control thyself in every way. This is the very essence of Yoga.

CHAPTER XVII

THE YOGA OF KNOWLEDGE

Śrī Krişņa (*continuing*):

I SHALL now tell thee of that knowledge revealed to the sages of old, acquiring which a man sees Truth as absolute, not as contingent upon a changing world, and knows himself free from that ignorance wherein he saw Truth modified by relative and finite values.

In the beginning, before there was any division of subject and object, there was one existence, Brahman alone, One without a second. That time is called the Kritayuga, or the golden age, when people skilled in knowledge and discrimination realized that one existence.

That one existence, the absolute reality, the Brahman, which transcends mind and speech, became divided into two, the Māyā, or the creative power, and the possessor of this power. Of these, one is known as Prakriti, which is cause as well as effect, and the other is called the Purusha, whose nature is self-luminous.

I am the Purusha. I willed, and there emanated from my Prakriti the Guṇas—Sattwa, Rajas, and Tamas. These contained within themselves the power to create, which produced Mahat, or universal intelligence. The universal intelligence underwent a process of change and gave forth the ego. And it is the ego which causes the delusion of manifoldness.

The ego, which is pure consciousness reflected through matter, is threefold, Sattwa, Rajas, and Tamas, which are respectively the causes of the evolution of mind, the senses, and the fine particles of matter.

Before the substances appeared as matter, they were in subtle form, and acting together formed an oval structure, which floated upon the water. In that oval structure I dwelt. From the centre of my being grew a lotus epitomizing the whole universe, and there the self-born Brahmā manifested himself.

Brahmā received my grace, and, endowed with Rajas, and by the power of his Tapas, he created the three spheres, Bhū, Bhuva, and Swa, together with their respective rulers.

The Swa became the abode of the gods; the Bhuva, that of the spirits; the Bhū, that of mortals. The spheres beyond the Swa became the abode of the Siddhas. Brahmā made the regions below Bhū, the earth, the abode of the Asuras and the Nāgas.

Works characterized by the three Guṇas lead to births in the different spheres. Good, pure, virtuous deeds lead one to the higher spheres and nobler births. But those who are entirely devoted to me transcend all spheres, and come at once to my being.

Through me—who am time and the ordainer of all things—all beings in the world, with their diverse karmas, rise and sink in the stream of the Guṇas. Whatever things or beings come into existence, minute or vast, slight or massive—all have their source in Purusha and Prakriti.

The substance from which a thing originates and into which it dissolves, abides also in the intermediate stage. That substance alone is real. The modifications have only a phenomenal and therefore a transitory and illusory existence.

Prakriti is the material cause of this manifested universe; Purusha is the substratum. Time is a factor in the modifications. Verily am I, Brahman, all three.

It is for the good of the soul that the varied modifications continue through an unbroken succession of cause and effect, until at last at the will of the Lord the universe ceases to exist.

Then the universe, which is pervaded by me, and which is the scene of births and deaths of multifarious beings, goes back to the state of dissolution. It goes back to me, the Ātman. The Ātman alone is the absolute reality.

As the rising sun dispels the darkness of the night, so the knowledge of the Ātman drives away all delusion.

CHAPTER XVIII

THE WORKING OF THE GUṆAS

Śrī Kriṣṇa (*continuing*):

O BEST of men, I shall tell thee now of the working and effects of the different Guṇas in their pure, unmixed forms. Listen attentively.

Poise, self-control, forbearance, discrimination, performance of one's duty, truthfulness, compassion, contentment, generosity, dispassion, faith and reverence, charity, the feeling of shame for ill conduct, and other such virtues, besides delight in the contemplation of the divine Self—these are the characteristics of Sattwa.

Lust, desire, strife, pride, haughtiness, prayer for selfish ends, self-aggrandizement, delight in sensuous things, picking of quarrels to feed vanity, love of fame, ridiculing of others, display of power, and aggressive enterprise—these are the characteristics of Rajas.

Anger, greed, lying, cruelty, begging, false piety, sloth, quarrelling, grief, infatuation, dejection, misery, sleep, expectation, fear, and inertia—these are the characteristics of Tamas.

Now listen to the effects of the mixed Guṇas.

The idea of "me" and "mine" comes from a mixture of all the Guṇas. All intercourse with the objective world through the mind, the sense organs, and the Prāṇas, is due to the mixture of the Guṇas.

When one is devoted to the performance of his duty, to the acquisition of wealth, to the satisfaction of legitimate desires, he is influenced by a mixture of the Guṇas. He attains faith, achieves material prosperity, devotes himself to family life, performs his duties faithfully, and becomes attached to the world.

One who has poise and self-control in a preponderant degree is endowed with Sattwa. He who is dominated by lust and selfish desire is influenced by Rajas. He who is given over to anger, greed, inertia, fear, and other evil passions, is governed by Tamas.

When a man worships me with devotion through works, without any selfish motive, he is of Sāttwika temperament. When one worships me through works for some self-gratification, he is of Rājasika temperament. And when one worships me desiring injury to others, he is of Tāmasika temperament.

The Guṇas—Sattwa, Rajas, and Tamas—belong to the Jīva, the individual soul, and affect not me, the true Self. They arise from the mind, and in the world of living beings the individuals who are attached to them become bound.

When Sattwa, which is pure and tranquil and which has the power to illumine, overcomes the other two Guṇas, then a man becomes endowed with happiness, virtue, and knowledge. When Rajas, which leads man to action, which rouses attachment, and causes the vision of multiplicity, overcomes Tamas and Sattwa, then a man becomes active, finds wealth and fame, and suffers misery. When

Tamas, which is characterized by inertia, and which casts a veil of ignorance over one's mind and makes one lose the power of discrimination, overcomes Rajas and Sattwa, then man becomes stricken with grief and delusion ; he lives in a dream of hope ; he becomes cruel ; he falls asleep spiritually.

A cheerful heart, subdued passions, a calm body, a mind unattached—know these to be the effects of Sattwa. Sattwa is the gateway to the realization of my being.

A restless heart, unsubdued passions, a body frenzied with desire for action, and a mind unquiet—know these to be the effects of Rajas.

A listless, stultified heart, a mind ignorant and dull, a body dejected and miserable—know these to be the effects of Tamas.

When Sattwa predominates, there is great illumination ; when Rajas predominates, there is intense activity ; and when Tamas predominates, there is unrelieved dullness.

Sattwa may be compared to the state of wakefulness, Rajas to dream, and Tamas to sleep. The Turiya—transcendental consciousness—persists in all three, and, since it is identical with the Self, is beyond them.

Sattwa leads gradually to higher and higher births upward to the sphere of Brahmā.

Tamas leads to lower births downward to vegetable life. Rajas operates to keep one within the circle of human births.

Meeting death when Sattwa is predominant, one goes to higher spheres : when Rajas is predominant, one comes back to the human plane, when Tamas is predominant, one is degraded to lower plane of existence. But those who have overcome the Guṇas verily attain to me.

Sāttwika is that deed which is done as service unto me, or without any desire for its fruits ; work done with a desire for fruits is Rājasa ; and cruel deeds are Tāmasa.

Higher intellectual knowledge is Sāttwika ; knowledge of physical science is Rājasa ; and knowledge common to the child and the ignorant is Tāmasa. Complete knowledge of me, the divine Self, is beyond the Guṇas.

To live in the forest amidst nature is Sāttwika-dwelling ; to live in a village or city is Rājasa-dwelling ; and to live in a gambling den is Tāmasa-dwelling. But to live in me is beyond the Guṇas.

The doer who is non-attached is Sāttwika ; one who is blinded by attachment is Rājasa ; and one who is reckless about consequences is Tāmasa. But one who has surrendered himself unto me is beyond the Guṇas.

Faith in the Self is Sāttwika ; faith in work is Rājasa ; faith in dishonesty is Tāmasa. But faith in service unto me is beyond the Guṇas.

Food which is wholesome, pure, and easily procurable is Sāttwika ; that which is merely palatable is Rājasa ; and that which is impure and injurious to health is Tāmasa.

Happiness arising from the contemplation of the Self is Sāttwika, that from objects of sense is Rājasa, and that from delusion and inertia is Tāmasa. But the happiness springing directly from knowledge of me is beyond the Guṇas.

Objects of sense, together with time, space, causation, knowledge, deed, doer, faith, state, and form are within the bounds of Guṇa. In short, whatever is seen, heard, or conceived by the mind and intellect is a modification of the Guṇas.

Man in bondage to the Guṇas remains subject to rebirth as regulated by the law of Karma. He who overcomes the Guṇas—which are only the manifestations of the mind in its relation to the world—and devotes himself to me with love, will attain to my being and realize freedom.

Let the wise man, therefore, blest as he is with this human birth, which is conducive to knowledge and realization, give up all attachment to the Guṇas and worship me. Let him, poised, self-controlled, freeing his mind from all distracting thoughts, worship me. By cultivating Sattwa alone he will overcome Rajas and Tamas. With complete tranquillity of mind let him then overcome Sattwa by Sattwa itself. A man thus freed from the bonds of the Guṇas is released from the ego, and attains to me.

A man freed from the ego, freed from the bonds of the Guṇas, freed thus from the limitations of the mind, finds fullness of life in me, the Brahman, the all-pervading existence. He is no longer subject to distractions from without arising from sensuous things, nor to troubled thoughts from within, caused by the wanderings of a restless mind.

CHAPTER XIX

THE FREE SOUL

Śrī Kriṣṇa (*continuing*) :

VERILY, having obtained human birth, which reflects my image, and having surrendered himself in love to me, a man ascends in his own being to me, the all-blissful, universal Self.

As the light of knowledge shines more and more steadily, a man becomes free from the false idea of individuality—the ego. Though he lives amidst Guṇas in this objective world —which is Māyā, an appearance—he does not become attached to the objects of the Guṇas, things of the senses. Absolute freedom is his. His heart is ever united with me. He is tranquil, and looks with an equal eye upon all. He has attachment to nothing, nor has he any ego; by going beyond the pairs of opposites he has attained peace.

His conversation is of me, listening to it, others become pure. For, hearing of me they acquire faith and become devoted to me. What more remains to be achieved by one who has learned to love me, who am Brahman—who am bliss and knowledge absolute, the repository of all blessed qualities?

Such a man is like a blazing fire, dispelling the gloom of darkness and burning the impurities of those about him. He who has realized Brahman is the supreme refuge of all. He is like a strong boat wherewith mortals may cross to immortality.

As food sustains life—as I, the Soul of all souls, am the refuge of the afflicted—and as virtue alone is treasure in the world to come —so is a free soul the refuge of those who seek release from birth and death.

The sun illumines earth and sky, but the saint, kindling the fire of divine wisdom, lights up the heart. He is the true friend of man. He is the Ātman. He is my very Self.

CHAPTER XX

REALIZATION OF GOD

Śrī Krişņa (*continuing*):

NEITHER praise the character and actions of any, nor dispraise them. Look upon the whole universe as an outgrowth of Purusha and Prakriti, and one with God.

He who praises or dispraises the character and actions of others has his heart set on the unreal, and therefore quickly falls away from the perfect spiritual state, wherein one sees God in all.

As, when the physical senses are overpowered by sleep and outward consciousness is lost, one dreams or sinks to utter forgetfulness, so in this finite world does one either dream the dream of universal life, or, seeing only manifoldness, wallow in darkness and delusion.

The finite world has no absolute reality. How, therefore, within its bounds, can there be any absolute good or any absolute evil?

Whatever is uttered by the tongue or conceived by the mind has no final reality.[1]

He who realizes the Lord God, the Ātman, the one existence, the Self of the universe, neither praises nor dispraises any man. Like the sun shining impartially upon all things, he looks with an equal eye upon all beings. He moves about in the world a free soul, released from all attachment.

Uddhava :

O Lord, for whom does this universe of relativity exist? It cannot exist for the

---

[1] The opening verses of this chapter and similar passages in Vedānta have sometimes been misunderstood. In the *Life of Śrī Rāmakrisṇa* we find mention of a pseudo-saint who lived for some time in the temple of Dakshineswar. This so-called saint used to teach and preach the unreality of the universe. But he was addicted to vice. One day Śrī Rāmakrisṇa asked him why he was so irresponsible and lived so licentiously, clothed as he was in the garb of a holy man. He replied, "Virtue and vice are both unreal, for the universe is unreal; and I am the Ātman. Nothing can touch me." To that Śrī Rāmakrisṇa replied, "If that is your Vedānta, I spit on Vedānta." The kind of misconstruction which this pseudo-saint had put upon the teachings of Vedānta is called in India "an indigestion of Vedānta".

It is true that Vedānta denies the reality of evil, and also of good : but what is denied is *absolute* not *relative*, reality. On the relative or finite plane, Vedānta holds that there are both good and evil, both virtue and vice, and that the individual man is wholly responsible for the quality of his deeds. On that plane the law of Karma inevitably obtains.

Ātman, for the Self is self-luminous, changeless, transcendent, pure ; neither can it exist for the body, which is a material object, devoid of intelligence. Nevertheless there is no denying that this relative existence *is*. For whom, then, does it exist ?

Śrī Krisṇa :

To the undiscriminating man, ignorant of his true Self, to one who identifies his Ātman with the body, senses, and Prāṇas, this relative existence, though it has no reality, appears real. As in a dream one seems to meet with actual experiences, so the ignorant man, immersed in illusion, mistakes shadow for substance.

As a dream seems to bring experience of many troubles to a man asleep but deludes him no longer when he wakes, so grief, joy, fear, anger, greed, infatuation, and all other emotions, as well as the experiences of birth and death, are felt to be real by the man who clings to the ego, but delude him no longer when he knows the Ātman, the true Self.

The individual man is the Ātman associated and identified with the body, the organs of sense, the Prāṇas, and the mind. Man is charaterized by his deeds and his Guṇas. As time goes on, he treads the round of birth and death.

Mind, speech, Prāṇas, body, and deeds, though they have no absolute reality, manifest diverse forms and characters. The wise man cuts asunder all attachment to these with the sword of knowledge, which is sharpened by worship of his Guru, and, thus delivered, he wanders at will over the face of the earth.

That alone which in the beginning was existence, and which alone in the end will be existence, and which alone is the cause and manifester of this universe—that only is absolute existence. How does one know this truth? One knows it by study of the Scriptures, by reasoning, by the practice of austerities, and by direct spiritual experience and insight.

As gold exists before it is made into ornaments, and will exist after the ornaments are melted away, and remains also as gold in the intermediate stage, when it is known by the various names of ornaments, so am I in relation to the universe—I was, I shall be, and I am.

The transcendental existence alone is real. Because of that existence the universe exists,[1] and that exists even when the universe ceases.

---

[1] "That shining, everything else shines." (The Katha Upanishad); "He is the Prāṇa of the Prāṇa, the eye of the eye." (The Brihad-Āraṇyaka Upanishad).

That which is neither in the beginning, nor in the end, but only in the middle, exists only in appearance. It is a mere name and form. Verily the experience that is caused and brought to light by the transcendental existence, which includes all, can be none other than that very existence.

Brahman is self-existent and self-effulgent. The universe of change was non-existent in the beginning, but because of the power in Brahman known as Rajas it appears as existent now.

Appearance is not reality : learn this from a wise teacher. Have recourse to the path that leads to the knowledge of Brahman, and removing all doubts about the Self, and detaching thyself from the senses, the seat of earthly desires, take delight in the blissful Self.

Discriminate between appearance and reality. The Ātman, the Self, is the reality, different from appearance, different from the body, the senses, the mind, the intellect, the ego, the subtle and gross elements.

To the man of realization, who has fully known my being, it is indifferent whether the senses—made up of the Guṇas—are indrawn or turned without. What matters it to the sun whether the clouds gather together or are dispersed ?

As ether remains unaffected by the changing seasons, so the invariable, indestructible Self, which is separate from the ego, remains untouched by the working of Sattwa, Rajas and Tamas. But man, identifying himself with the Guṇas, treads the round of birth and death.

Contact with the things of this world, which are the creation of Māyā, should be avoided until attachment, which is a stain on the mind, has been removed through devotion to me.[1]

As a malady, if not treated properly, comes back again and again to trouble a man, so attachment and tendencies formed in the mind by past habits, if not wiped out completely, torment a Yogin by their recurrence as he comes into contact with the objective world.

Indeed, even the Devas are jealous of a Yogin, striving as he does to surpass them by attaining Brahman. They therefore try to lead him astray, in various ways, if they find him off his guard. But if because of accumulated tendencies created by past habits,

---

[1] The point may be thus expressed : Though it is true that no stain can attach itself to the ever-pure Ātman, we must not think that we can act in any way we please. Before we can rise above merit and demerit we must attain purity of heart by learning self-control and self-restraint, and then alone is the Ātman realized as ever-pure.

and also because of the subtle influence of the Devas, a Yogin is not entirely successful in his efforts to free his heart from attachment, in the next life he will succeed and attain the goal of Yoga. His struggles in this life will bear fruit in the next.

The ignorant man, attached to his body, is controlled by the impressions and tendencies created by his past deeds, and is bound by the law of Karma. But the wise man, his desires being quenched, is not affected by deeds. He is beyond the law of Karma. Since his mind rests in the Ātman he is not affected by the conditions which surround him, though he may continue to live in the body and though his senses may move amongst sense objects. For he has realized the vanity of all objects, and in multiplicity sees one infinite Lord. He is like to a man who has awakened from sleep and learned that his dream was a dream.

In ignorance alone, before one finds illumination, the diversified deeds, which are the workings of the Guṇas, seem to attach themselves to the Self. With the dawn of knowledge they clear away. The Ātman, however, remains unaffected, for neither in ignorance does it become impure with deeds, nor in knowledge does it become free from impurity. The Ātman itself is ever pure.

As the rising sun dispels darkness from men's eyes and discovers what before lay hidden, so the dawn of knowledge removes evil from men's intellect and reveals the Ātman. Then do men know themselves as the Ātman, and the Ātman as themselves.

The Ātman is self-luminous and birthless; it is existence, absolute knowledge, the eye of the eyes, one without a second. It is beyond speech. Because of its existence all bodily powers perform their functions. The finite, multiple universe has no existence apart from the infinite Self. The finite is the reading of finitude into the infinite. Seeing the finite in the infinite Self is a delusion of the mind.

This self-existent Self is to be realized by the practices of Yoga. Should the body of a Yogin who is following the path of Yoga and is not yet an adept be overtaken by disease, he must heal himself by such remedies as concentration, breathing exercises, posture, austerities, and Mantrams, as well as by medicine. Mental diseases such as lust, desire, egotism, vanity, are to be cured by meditating on me, by chanting my name, and by serving great teachers. Some misguided people there are who practise Yoga to obtain health and perpetual youth, and to acquire extraordinary powers; but by the wise such action is not approved. Indeed, such action is vain, since life is mortal. One should desire health and strength only as a means of serving me and attaining to my being.

The Yogin who practises this Yoga, surrendering himself unto me and having no other desire but me, is thwarted by nothing. His is a bliss that fades not away.

CHAPTER XXI

UDDHAVA GOES TO BADARIKĀŚRAMA

Uddhava (*addressing Śrī Krişṇa*) :

I CONSIDER this Yoga extremely difficult to follow for one who is not a master of his senses. Pray teach me in a simple way how a man may easily attain the highest end.

Often, O Lotus-eyed one, a struggling soul is seized with despondency. For one who does not surrender himself in love to thee fails to find tranquility and in the vain effort to do so becomes exhausted.

Hence, O Lord of the universe, sages who have realized the spirit of religion take shelter with a cheerful heart at thy Lotus Feet, which bestow ineffable joy. Such as these the inscrutable power of Māyā cannot bind.

O thou Friend of all, verily dost thou give thyself unreservedly to thy devotees, who have no other refuge but thee. Even though gods and angels, or the great monarchs of the earth, heap up treasures and crowns at thy Feet, still art thou a friend of the lowly and humble.

O thou beloved Lord, the Self of all, thou dost fulfil the desire of those who take refuge in thee. Knowing how thou dost love thy lovers, who could resist loving thee? If one man desires only worldly happiness and prosperity, and another desire to be free from these, thou art equally their refuge. Whom else but thee would they worship? What indeed is inaccessible to them who adore the very dust that thy Feet tread?

Thou art the Guru without, thou art the Self within, thou removest the blemishes of the heart and revealest thy kingdom to thy devotees. None can repay his debt of gratitude to thee. The very thought of thy grace fills the heart with ever-increasing joy.

Śrī Krișņa :

Now I shall tell thee of spiritual practices which are easy to follow. If a mortal practises them sincerely, verily will he conquer invincible death.

With thy heart tranquil, keep me in constant remembrance while performing thy duties as service unto me, surrender thyself to me heart and soul, and thou shalt find joy in following my path. Live in the society of holymen, my devotees, and imitate their conduct. With thy heart purified, see me, the all-pervadiing Ātman, in thyself and in the hearts of all other beings.

O noble soul, open thy divine sight and regard and honour all beings as myself. Wise is he who looks with an equal eye upon all beings, seeing the one indwelling God in the hearts of all. He who meditates on my divine nature as present in every man becomes free from rivalry, from jealousy, from hatred, and from the consciousness of ego.

One who has realized Brahman sees Brahman everywhere and in all. To look upon all beings as myself, and to shape one's conduct towards them accordingly, in thought, word and deed—that is the best method of worship. Such is the wisdom of the wise, and the insight of the intelligent by which in this very birth—this illusory and fleeting existence—one may reach even to me, the real and the eternal.

I have told thee the excellent truth of Brahman, knowing which a man has his doubts dispelled and attains to freedom.

To one who fully communicates this knowledge to my devotees I freely give myself, for he imparts thereby the supreme knowledge. He himself becomes purified by holding aloft the lamp of knowledge and by thus revealing me to others. Moreover, the man who every day calmly listens to the sacred and purifying truths of the Self, with reverent heart and with devotion to me—he also is not fettered by the bondage of life.

Friend Uddhava, has thou rightly comprehended Brahman? Art thou free from infatuation and from grief?

For him who has truly known Brahman, there is nothing to learn. He who has quenched his thirst with nectar craves no other drink.

When a man relinquishing all attachment, surrenders himself to me, he realizes his oneness with me and attains to immortality.

When Uddhava was thus taught the path of Yoga, and had listened to the very words of the glorious Śrī Krişṇa, his eyes filled with tears of gratitude, and his voice choked with love. He remained silent, with folded palms.

He felt himself supremely blessed, and having controlled his feelings he touched the Lotus Feet of Krişṇa with his head, and, his palms folded, thus began:

Uddhava :

Thy very presence, O Lord of the universe, has removed delusion from my heart. Can the chill of darkness and fear overcome him who stands by a fire ?

Thou hast of thy grace restored to me, thy servant, the lamp of knowledge. How can he who knows thy grace forsake thee and seek another ?

Obeisance unto thee, O great Yogin ! and be thou pleased to tell me, who have taken refuge in thee, how I may grow in devotion to thy Lotus Feet.

Śrī Krisṇa

Go, Uddhava, at my command, to my hermitage called Badarikā, where at the very sight of the Alakanandā, the sacred river that sprang from my Feet, all thy sins, O beloved friend, will be washed away, and by bathing in its waters, or by merely touching them, thou shalt be purified. There, clad in bark, living on wild roots and fruits, averse to pleasures, patient under all hardships, calm and poised, with thy senses under control and thy mind concentrated, possessed of knowledge and realization, reflecting on what I have told thee and thou hast well learned, with thy speech and mind directed towards me follow my path. Thus shalt thou transcend the limitations of the three Guṇas and attain to me, the supreme.

Thus addressed by him the very thought of whom charms away the delusion of earthly existence, Uddhava, before taking leave, placed his head at his Lotus Feet and bathed them with tears of love ; for though he had risen above earthly pleasure and pain, his heart was gripped with sorrow at the thought of separation from his beloved Kriṣṇa. Only with extreme effort could he bring himself to leave him. At last, saluting Kriṣṇa again and again, and crowning himself with the master's slippers,[1] he went away.

Then, enshrining Śrī Kriṣṇa in the inner sanctuary of his heart, Uddhava journeyed to Badarikā, and following the teachings of his Guru, the one friend of the universe, this great devotee attained oneness with the Lord Hari, the God of Love.

He who but tastes with genuine faith and love this nectar of knowledge which was bestowed on the devoted Uddhava by Śrī Kriṣṇa, whose Feet the masters of Yoga worship, frees himself and the world with him.

---

[1] The act was symbolic of his humble devotion.

That revealer of the Scriptures, who, to free us from the fear of birth and death, extracted for us the essence of knowledge, the very nectar of wisdom, from the wide sea of the Vedas, and then gave this wisdom to his servants that they might drink as at the fountain of life ; that primal, eternal, and perfect being, known to all as Śrī Kriṣṇa—him I salute !

BOOK TWELFTH

THE ARGUMENT

THE Sūta tells of the conversation regarding immortality that took place between Śuka and King Parīkṣit, and of King Parīkṣit's death.

CHAPTER I

ŚUKA TEACHES PARĪKSIT DIVINE WISDOM

Śuka (*to King Parīkṣit*):

O KING, blessed are they who meditate on the indwelling God, for they shall be pure. Blessed indeed are they who worship God in the sanctuary of their hearts, who chant his name, and pray to him, and sing his glory, for they shall be clean of all evil. As gold is freed from dross by fire, so the heart of man is freed from evil desires by meditation on the all-pervading Lord residing within the soul.

O king, that thou shalt ever die is not true. It is causeless fear. Therefore have courage. The body alone has a beginning and an end : thou art beyond the body, and greater than it. For thee there is no death.

Thou art immortal, not as the seed lives in the tree, nor as a man lives in his children and his children's children, but in thy Self as a being distinct from the body—distinct as the fire is from the wood. The Ātman, separate from the body, is birthless and deathless.

Beyond death art thou, and unchangeable.

Be discriminative and know thy true Self.

Think thou on the Self, the all-pervading existence.

" I am the supreme Brahman " : thus meditating, realize thy oneness with God. No death can do thee harm. On death shalt thou place thy feet.

Śuka, the knower of Brahman, taught this Wisdom of God to King Parīkṣit. The king, having listened to it, prostrated himself before Śuka, and, with folded palms, said :

"Master, blessed am I. I am grateful to thee. Out of the kindness of thy heart thou hast revealed to me the supreme kindness and sympathy for mankind, who suffer the miseries of the world.

"Thou hast revealed the sacred Scripture which speaks of divine glory and of divine love and of divine knowledge. No more do I fear death, for thou hast shown me the way to the fearless realm of Brahman.

"I have learned what is to be known. With thy blessing I will now control my senses, and concentrate my mind, with all its desires and ambitions, on the Lotus Feet of Śrī Krişṇa, my chosen Avatāra, the door which leads to the vision of God and to union with Brahman, the all-pervading existence.

"Free am I from all delusion ; firmly established am I in knowledge. Thou has shown me the way to the supreme good."

The pure, the ever-free, the wise Śuka, together with the other holy men of the assembly, took his departure from the king. King Parīkşit sat facing north on the bank of the sacred river Ganges. He, the great Yogi, silenced his turbulent senses and became deeply absorbed in meditation on his chosen Avatāra, the Soul of all souls. Eventually he became free from physical consciousness, and his mind was united with Brahman.

The curse of the young Brahmin—that the king should die of snake-bite—was about to take effect. The hour had come when the king was to give up his body and attain absolute freedom. Now, true to the prediction, Takshaka, the king of serpents, appeared, and poured his venom into the king's body, which then was dissolved back into the elements from which it came.

EPILOGUE

THE Sūta brings to an end his long discourse before the company of sages by proclaiming the glories of the *Bhāgavatam*.

EPILOGUE

THE Sūta concluded his relation of the *Bhāgavatam* to the sages in the forest with the following words :

" Ever new and ever inspiring are the teachings of the sacred *Bhāgavatam*. Meditation on the divine life of Śrī Krişņa is elevating ; it charms away the sorrows of life and leads one to realization of the God of Love. To chant his name is sanctifying. Constant remembrance of the Lotus Feet of Śrī Krişņa purifies the heart, drives away evil, nourishes true love and supremest wisdom.

" O ye saints, best and noblest are ye of men, for within the sanctuaries of your hearts ye constantly meditate on and worship him who is the Soul of all souls.

" Having come to this sacred hermitage, and into your holy society, I have remembered the truth of God which I heard directly from the lips of Śuka in the assemly of saints before King Parīkşit.

" This *Bhāgavatam* that I have faithfully repeated to you is the essence of the Vedānta.

One who reads or devoutly harkens to its teachings is freed from all evil and instructed in wisdom. Very dear is it to the lovers of God. With all reverence is it studied by the knowers of Brahman. The truths which it contains are indeed pure; and they purify all whom they touch!

"In the beginning of time the truths contained herein were revealed to Brahmā, the first-born. Brahmā held the lamp of knowledge before Nārada and Vyāsa. Vyāsa kindled the fire of Truth in the heart of his son Śuka, the great Yogi. Śuka carried the sacred light to King Parīkṣit.

"May we meditate on Brahman, pure, sorrowless, immortal, the source of all revelation!

"Our obeisance to Śrī Krisṇa, the God of Love!

"Our salutation to Śuka, the prince of Yogis!"

OM......Śrī Rāmakriṣṇārpaṇam astu.
OM......PEACE. PEACE. PEACE.

GLOSSARY
OF
SANSKRIT TERMS

Agni. (1) Fire. (2) God of fire. (3) One of the presiding deities of the sense-organs.

Ājnā. The centre of spiritual consciousness behind the space between eyebrows.

Anāhata. The centre of spiritual consciousness in the heart.

Āśrama. (1) A place of spiritual retreat. (2) A stage of life—that of student, house-holder, hemit, of monk.

Ashṭānga Yoga. The path of Rājayoga, consisting of eight steps : (1) Practice of the moral virtues : harmlessness, truthfulness, non-stealing, continence, and freedo from greed. (2) Regular habits of outward and inward purity, contentment, austerity, study, and self-surrender to God. (3) Posture. (4) Control of Prāṇa through the practice of breathing exercises. (5) Withdrawal of the mind from sense objects. (6) Concentration. (7) Meditation (8) Absorption in the consciousness of God.

Asura. Demons, who are in perpetual hostility to the gods or Devas.

Atharva. One of the four Vedas.

Ātman. The Self in man, which is identical with God.

Avadhūta. Mendicant.

Avatāra. A manifestation of God as a man—for example, Rāma, Krisṇa, Christ.

Avidyā. The veil of ignorance which covers the Self within.

Avidyā-māyā. (See Avidyā).

Avyakta. The universe in its unmanifested state—that is, the material cause of the universe, composed of three forces called Guṇa. (See Guṇa).

Bhagavān. (1) God. (2) Epithet used for an Avatāra, *q.v.*

Bhakti. Love, devotion.

Bhakti-yoga. The path of devotion.

Bhāratavarsha. India.

Bhū. Earth.

Bhuva. Sky.

Brahmā. One of the Hindu trinity, the Creator.

Brahma-loka. The heaven of Brahmā.

Brahman. God in his impersonal, absolute aspect.

Brahmin. (1) The highest of the four Hindu castes. (2) A member of the highest caste.

Devas. Gods, celestial beings.

Dharma. (1) Duty. (2) Virtue. (3) Law.

Dwija. One who is "twice-born."

Gandharvas. Celestial musicians inhabiting Indra's heaven.

Gāyatri mantra. The sacred verse from the Ṛg Veda meditated upon by all Hindus but those of the lowest caste : " May we meditate on the effulgent Light of him who is worshipful, and who has given birth to all worlds. May he direct the rays of our intelligence towards the paṭh of good."

Gopī. Shepherdess of Brindāvan and playmate of Krisṇa.

Guṇa. The Guṇas are three in number : Sattwa, Rajas and Tamas. These are the forces or substances which constitute Prakriti or Avyakta, the material cause of the universe of mind and matter. The Guṇas, therefore, are the components of every object, including the mind of man. Sattwa expresss itself psychologically as tranquillity, purity, calmness ; Rajas as passion, restlessness, aggressive activity ; Tamas as stupidity, laziness, inertia. Sometimes one Guṇa is predominant, sometimes another. A man is either benevolent or malevolent, tranquil or restless, active or lazy, saintly or wicked, according as one or another Guṇa is predominant. But he can cultivate by his actions and thoughts and by his way of living anyone of the Guṇas. It is taught that Tamas is to be overcome by the cultivation of Rajas, and Rajas is to be overcome by the cultivation of Sattwa. The ultimate ideal is to go beyond Sattwa also and attain to the Ātman, which is beyond and above the Guṇas.

Guru. Spiritual master, one who teaches the secrets of meditation.

Hamsa. (1) (Literally) Swan. (2) (Figuratively) the Self.

Hara. (See Śiva).

Hari. One who steals the hearts of mankind —the eternal beloved God.

Indra. The king of the gods.

Ishṭam. Any concept under which an individual chooses to worship God.

Jana loka. One of the seven divisions of the world, the region where the sons of Brahmā and other pious men reside.

Japam. The practice of repeating a sacred syllable (a name of God) as taught by a Guru.

Jātismara. One who is born with the power of recollecting his preceding incarnation.

Jina. One who has conquered his mind and is therefore self-controlled.

Jīva. An individual being—the Self in association with the mind, the senses and the body.

Karma. (1) Deed. (2) Effect of a deed. (3) Law of causation operating on the mental and moral plane.

Keśava. Krisṇa.

Kinnara. A demigod, with a human figure and the head of a horse, attached to the service of Kubera as a celestial chorister or musician.

Krita yuga. Golden age.

Kshatriya. (1) The warrior caste. (2) A member of the warrior caste.

Kuśa. Sacred dry grass.

Loka. A division of the universe. (According to the Hindus the universe is made up of many Lokas, each of which is inhabited by various orders of beings.)

Mahat. Cosmic intelligence, a product of the Guṇas.

Maṇipūra. The centre of spiritual consciousness situated in the solar plexus.

Mantram. A sacred name of God to be meditated upon.

Māyā. (1) The power of God that creates, preserves, and dissolves the universe. (2) Spiritual ignorance that prevails except in illumined souls. (3) That which is ephemeral.

Muni. (1) Seer. (2) Thinker.

Nara-Nārāyaṇa. Krisṇa, the incarnation of Vishṇu.

Niyama. Regular habits of outward and inward purity, contentment, austerity, study, and self-surrender to God.

Pitri. " The manes, or the deceased and deified progenitors of mankind, inhabiting a peculiar region or heaven, or according to some, the orbit of the moon." Horace Haymon Wilson : *Sanskrit-English Dictionary*.

Prakriti. Primordial nature. (See Guṇa).

Prāṇa. Vital energy.

Prāṇāyāma. Control of vital energy through the practice of breathing exercise as taught in yoga philosophy.

Prārabdha. That portion of the impressions of the deeds done in previous lives which has begun to take effect in the present life.

Pratyāhāra. Withdrawal of the mind from sense objects.

Pura. (1) City. (2) Body.

Purusha. The Self (literally, " dweller in the body ").

Rajas. One of the three Guṇas. (See Guṇa).

Rājasa. Of the nature of Rajas.

Rājasika. Of the nature of Rajas.

Rākshasa. Demon.

Rik. (1) Hymn. (2) One of the four Vedas.

Rishi. Seer.

Sahasrāra. The centre of spiritual consciousness in the brain.

Sāma. One of the four Vedas.

Samādhi. Transcendental consciousness.

Sāmkhya. (1) Spiritual knowledge. (2) Name of one of the six systems of Indian philosophy.

Sannyāsa. The vow of renunciation.

Sannyāsin. One who takes the vow of renunciation.

Sattwa. One of the three Guṇas. (See Guṇa).

Sāttwika. Of the nature of Sattwa.

Satya Loka. The abode of Brahmā—the highest sphere amongst the divisions of the world.

Satchidānanda. Absolute existence, absolute knowledge, absolute bliss—referring to God in his absolute, impersonal aspect.

Śakti. (1) Power of God. (2) God the Mother.

Śiva. (1) Absolute good. (2) One of the gods of the Hindu trinity.

Śūdra. (1) The lowest caste. (2) A member of the lowest caste.

Siddhas. Demigods inhabiting the region between the earth and the sun.

Sphota. Logos.

Sthāvara. Stationary beings, such as herbs and plants.

Sushumnā. The canal in the centre of the spine through which the spiritual energy flows in exalted states.

Swa. Sky—the division of the universe between the sun and the polar star.

Tamas. One of the three Guṇas. (See Guṇa).

Tāmasa. Of the nature of Tamas.

Tāmasika. Of the nature of Tamas.

Tapas. Austerity, meditation.

Turīya. Transcendental consciousness.

Vaikuṇṭha. Heaven—the abode of Vishṇu.

Vaiśya. (1) one of the four castes—the commercial. (2) A member of the commercial caste.

Varsha. Land, country.

Vidyādharas. Demigods inhabiting the air.

Vidyā Māyā. The power of good that leads a man toward liberation.

Viṇā. A musical instrument having steel strings stretched on a long fretted fingerboard over two gourds.

Vishṇu. God in his aspect as preserver and ruler of the universe.

Viśuddha. The centre of spiritual consciousness situated back of the throat—called the "throat centre".

Yajur. One of the four Vedas.

Yama. Practice of the moral virtues ; harmlessness, truthfulness, non-stealing, continence, and freedom from greed.

Yoga. (1) Union with God. (2) Path to union with God.

Yoga, Eightfold. The eight steps of the Yoga path as taught by Patanjali. (See Ashtānga Yoga).

Yoga powers. Occult powers (see pp. 245-6).

Yogi. One who follows the Yoga path.

Yogin. Another form of the word Yogi.

Yuga. Cycle. (See footnote, page 13).